THE MAKING
OF A PEACE CORPS
VOLUNTEER

FROM MAINE TO THAILAND

ROGER O. PARENT

Don
Have a good
read. Roger

THE MAKING
OF A PEACE CORPS
VOLUNTEER

FROM MAINE TO THAILAND

Publisher: ZRS BOOKS

Copyright © 2013 by Roger O. Parent

ISBN 978-0-9889769-0-0

For orders and information please contact
Roger O. Parent
814 Marietta Street
South Bend, Indiana 46601
Email: rogerop@gmail.com
1-574-233-5753

Website: www.rogerparent.org

Designed by: Donald Nelson
Edited by: James E. Wensits

(All names of Thai nationals have been changed. Except for a few public persons, I use first names or initials.)

Preface

I'm writing in a small room in my small house in South Bend, Indiana, where I arrived in 1964 from two years of volunteering in Peace Corps in Thailand. I'm writing stories from my first twenty-four years.

I'm writing for many reasons, one not more important than another: I'm writing for the enjoyment of reflection and writing; I'm writing for the enjoyment of my children and other kindred spirits; I'm writing for a better understanding of myself . . . and if readers get pleasure and understand their lives better by reflecting on mine, that would please me.

Mine is a story of overcoming the critical illness of my first months to robust health; of living in Acadian French-speaking Northern Maine to immersion in Thailand; of learning French in my village to learning English in school to learning Thai in Thailand; of growing from deep shyness to the openness required of a Peace Corps teacher; of moving from an adherence to the externalities of my Catholic religion to a deeper faith in life and in God.

Life is what we do and what happens to us, and my stories are about what I've done and what's happened to me. I write stories suggestive of my growth and development from a nascent sense of self and consciousness embedded at birth to the end of my service as a member of the first group of Peace Corps Volunteers in Thailand (Thailand 1), from 1961 to 1963.

Many paths lay before me at birth. My sense of self, my consciousness – a gift from the gods – was merely a seed, or an innate thrust, or a friendly shove toward a greater consciousness; it had to be nurtured by my parents, elicited by my teachers, and supported by my community. Ultimately, though, it was up to me to develop this sacred gift, to create my life; I had to act and to react, I had to experience and to learn from the world that was given to me.

These are my stories to age 24.

Maine

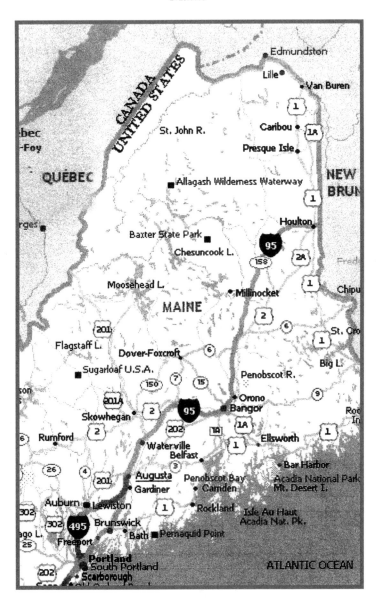

Thailand

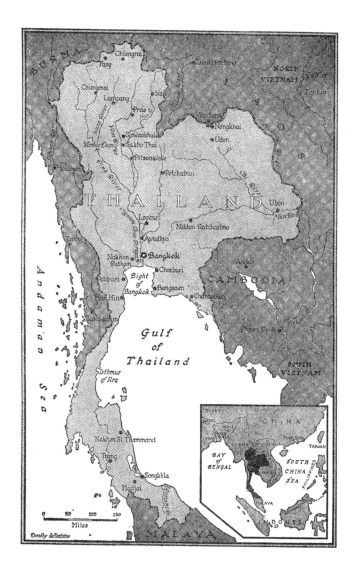

Part I

GROWING UP IN LILLE, MAINE

January 22, 1939

My parents had six children and could not afford another child...or maybe they didn't want another child, but I don't know that. This was during the end of the Depression. They had lost their savings, jobs were still scarce, and birth control was an inexact science fraught with moral implications for my parents, who were very devout Catholics. They tried to follow the birth control allowed by the Church: abstinence, nursing the last baby as long as possible, and having sexual intercourse only when they thought my mother was not fertile. But nothing worked and I was born January 22, 1939, on a very cold day in Lille, a small village in Northern Maine, a few hundred yards from the border with New Brunswick, Canada.

After I was born, my parents, although not naturally superstitious, tried the birth control method of an old French Acadian tale: if you named the seventh child after the grandfathers or grandmothers, this would be your last child. I was the seventh child, and my parents, desperate not to have another, named me Jean Octave Roger. Unfortunately for my parents, and fortunately for my three

1

younger sisters, this birth control didn't work. Years later, toward the end of her long life, my mother told me, "If I were young, I would not follow the Church's ban on artificial [whatever that means] birth control."

My father, Noel Parent, had driven three miles in the middle of the night through swirling snow in his Model T Ford for Dr. Faucher to assist my delivery. Dr. Faucher would have willingly driven to our house, but we had no telephone to call him, and the few with telephones in Lille were sleeping. Anyway, my father didn't like to speak on the telephone; he would even drive long distances to avoid doing so, but this was a short drive.

When Dr. Faucher arrived, he probably thought he could have stayed home in his warm bed, because my Memére (Acadian French for grandmother) Corbin was preparing for my imminent delivery – Memére was a midwife who substituted for Dr. Faucher in many deliveries. I must have felt blessed to have Memére present at my birth.

I would like to remember how it felt to be born. There I was in the womb, the only world I knew – warm and squishy and comfortable – when suddenly I was pushed out into a cold, hard, and foreign world, as if I was not wanted anymore. Later, I hope much later, after I've made the best of this life, I will be thrust out of this world into another world. Maybe dying is like being born.

THE SISTERS PRAY FOR ME

I weighed seven pounds at six weeks and seven pounds at six months. I cried constantly, night and day. Nothing could stop my crying: not being held and lullabied by my mother, not being held and danced by my father, not being held and rocked by my sisters, and not being cuddled by Memére Corbin. Not even Mrs. Anna B. could soothe me; this good neighbor, to relieve my mother, cared for me in her house one night; I cried so hard she thought I would die in her arms.

Something was wrong with me that no one could remedy: our Dr. Faucher from Grand-Isle couldn't cure me; Dr. Hammond from Van Buren couldn't cure me; not even Memére Corbin, who practiced a sort of folk medicine, could find a cure for me. Someone thought I was not getting nourishment from my mother's milk and suggested cow's milk, or canned milk, but nothing worked. An old neighbor suggested massaging my body with olive oil, figuring I would get nutrition by osmosis, but that only relaxed me . . . and that was good.

Meanwhile, everyone was praying for me. My father and mother prayed, my brothers and sisters prayed, my aunts and uncles prayed, my cousins and neighbors prayed, and my pastor prayed; but most of all, the Daughters of Wisdom Sisters prayed for me. My father and mother believed in the power of prayer: my mother attended mass almost daily and said the rosary in family every evening; they were people of prayer. But even prayer didn't seem to work for me.

My parents and older siblings were deeply worried and anguished. They had consulted many doctors and had prayed to many saints, but I was weakening and they feared I wouldn't live much longer. In desperation my mother and father took me to another doctor, I think in Grand Falls, New Brunswick, some forty miles away – a long distance in those days – but like the others, he had no cure for me. He thought I had just a few more days to live. My mother and father returned home brokenhearted thinking this was it: I was going to die.

My father, not one to give up easily, decided to visit the good Sisters again. Prayer was all he had left and he believed the prayers of Sisters reached God more directly than his. He and my mother knew well the Daughters of Wisdom: they called on him often to repair this and that; my mother had been educated from kindergarten through high school by the Sisters, and my siblings were being taught by them. My mother's cousin, Patrick Theriault, had invited the Sisters to Lille from Quebec, and my mother's father, Jean Corbin, had paddled them in his canoe across the St. John River to Lille in 1905. The sisters would do anything for my family.

Soeur (Sister) Agnes du Sauveur answered the door to the convent and knew from the look on my father's face that my situation was grim. She promised my father they would start praying for me immediately, and would pray through the night, each Sister taking her turn in the chapel. They would implore their Founder, Saint Louis-Marie de Montfort, to intercede with God for my cure.

The morning after my father visited Soeur Agnes, he had a small carpentry job to do at Phillip D.'s house in Grand-Isle, three miles away. When he got there, tired from another night of my crying, he shared the details of my illness with Mrs. D. He said everything possible had been done and his only hope was for a miracle. It was up to the saints – the holy people – and God.

While Mrs. D. was preparing lunch for her family it came to her that the symptoms my father had described were very similar to those of her oldest son, who her mother had cured with a remedy given to her by an old lady, now deceased. She hurried to my father, working in the basement, to tell him of her son and the remedy. If my father was interested she would ask her mother, who lived nearby, if she still had the remedy.

My father, willing to try anything, grabbed this last straw. Mrs. D.'s mother remembered the remedy and my father left immediately to purchase lactic acid at the pharmacy in Madawaska, some twelve miles away, and Karo syrup at Lawrence's General Store in Lille. There was no time to lose; I was on the edge of death.

My father rushed home, got a quart of our cow's milk from the deep well where it was kept cold, poured it in a glass bowl, stoked the fire in the wood-burning stove, brought the milk to its boiling point, and let it cool. My eldest sister, Noella, stirred 100 drops of lactic acid in the milk with a wooden spoon. (The wooden spoon and glass bowl were used because the acid would have reacted with metal.) Karo syrup was added to sweeten the bitter milk and my mother enlarged the holes in the rubber nipple to make it easier for me to suckle the thickened, curdled milk. Now, evening had arrived. My mother fed me a bottle of the remedied milk, laid me in the small crib in her room, and went to bed, tired from the work, and emotionally drained.

When my parents woke up next morning, they thought I was dead, because I hadn't awakened them with my crying. My mother was so sure of it that she sent my father to check on me. He got up, walked to my crib expecting the worst, but I was breathing and sleeping peacefully. Tears ran down his face. I had slept through a night for the first time since my birth. The house was jubilant, and word of my cure ran throughout the school and the village. On his way to work that morning, my father stopped by the convent to tell the Sisters of Mrs. D., of the lactic acid and the Karo syrup, and of my first full night's sleep. "It was a miracle," he said, "a miracle their prayers had wrought."

My mother fed me this miracle milk, and in two months I had attained the normal weight of an eight-month-old . . . and my mother had gained back some pounds as well. Later – I don't know when – I was able to digest untreated cows' milk, and I've been enjoying milk ever since.

My family believed that God had influenced Phillip D. to hire my father for a small job that day and had given Mrs. D. the patience to listen to my distracted father's story, and that God had been influenced by the prayers, especially the prayers of the Sisters. The doctors had not been able to cure me with their science; Memére had not been able to cure me with her folk medicine, and the warm loving care of my parents had not been enough. The Sisters' special prayers to Saint Louis-Marie de Montfort for intervention with God had cured me.

Everyone in Lille believed my cure was a miracle. I believe it was a miracle too, but not in the traditional sense of the word. I believe in prayer, I believe in community prayer, I believe all people are connected across geography and across time, and I believe we're all joined to powers we don't know and don't understand. When we pray, when we beseech these unknown powers, we draw on their strength, and they respond to us. We may call these powers God and we may call their responses miracles, but miracles are what happen when we pray and work together for good causes.

MY SCHOOL OUTHOUSE

One cold January day when I was in kindergarten, I had to go to the outhouse to relieve myself during the school day. I didn't mind urinating in the school outhouse, even though the stink was awful, but I didn't care to sit on the dirty rim of the outhouse bench seat.

Notre Dame du Mont Carmel elementary school had been converted from an old Catholic church in 1908 or so, when a new and much larger church was built. There were five classrooms in the school – three on the first floor and two on the second floor. The new church, a chapel, the Sisters' convent, and the old church building – now a school – were connected to each other. Appended to this ensemble were the toilet facilities housed in what looked like two little houses which jutted outside the main building. These little houses were big outhouses, one for boys and one for girls. They were different from a regular outhouse in their size and in their being connected to the school – we didn't have to walk outside to use them. Outhouses were not heated and were extremely cold and uncomfortable during the winter, especially when you consider their function.

When I started school in 1945, outhouses were not uncommon to many homes in Lille. My home had an outhouse attached to our small barn, and we had a chamber pot in the house which we emptied morning and evening. For many years after we had a flush toilet, when I was about four, we continued using the outhouse during summer. And in all seasons, we boys (and grown men, too) peed behind the barn. In winter we had contests to see who could make the farthest pee mark in the snow. (Indecent exposure was not a factor; no one lived within a hundred miles from our barn.)

It was way below zero that day; it was so cold hot pee froze before hitting the pile of dung below. Young boys were not accurate, and a huge ridge of frozen yellow pee had accumulated on the rim – it was inches thick. Not only was the air ghastly cold, but to sit on iced pee was beyond me.

I returned to the classroom squeezing my buttocks so tightly I could barely walk. But after fifteen minutes or so, I had to go. I told Sister Simeon, my kindergarten teacher, that I was sick and had to go home. She let me go, seeing in my anxious face and squirming body that something was wrong with me. She helped with my boots and coat and I started running home. But I had waited too long and could not hold it any longer; stuff started coming out of my body and I started bawling. I was crying more out of embarrassment than out of discomfort from what was slowly congealing and freezing in my pants.

When I reached home, I didn't tell my mother what had happened, but she could smell me, knew what had happened, and didn't coax it out of me. She was relieved to know I wasn't sick and I was relieved she didn't scold me. Most important, she did not force me to return to school that day, nor did she mention this incident during the evening conversations. She knew how embarrassed I felt.

CUSSING SISTER SIMEON IN FRENCH

Cussing Sister Simeon in any language was not a good idea, but doing so in French was even worse. Sister Simeon was my kindergarten teacher, and one of her main tasks was to teach English to me and the other students.

I entered kindergarten speaking only French – Acadian French – as did the other children in Lille. The people of Lille were, and most still are, descendants of French-speaking peoples from New Brunswick, Quebec, and Nova Scotia (Named L'Acadie by its French Founders). The Acadian French I spoke with mixed-in English words made for a unique mélange of words and accents.

My parents knew how to speak English, but I never heard them speak it together. They spoke English only when they had to speak with an "outsider," which didn't happen often. It was the same in every other Lille home. We spoke French until we left for work in cities such as Boston and Hartford, or for the Armed Services, or for University.

When I was six years old, the only radio station we could pull in easily was a French language station (CJEM) about twelve miles away in Edmundston, New Brunswick.

When I was about twelve, an English language radio station opened in Caribou, Maine, and an English language television station opened in Presque Isle, Maine. But in Lille, we continued listening to CJEM, and continued watching French language television from St. John, New Brunswick.

Sister Simeon was old and losing patience, and I was young and had not yet found patience. One day she was trying to teach English words: chair for chaise, snow for neige, window for fenêtre, and I was not paying attention. I didn't want to speak English. She got upset and scolded me harshly. I got upset and whispered, thinking she wouldn't hear, "Mange de la merde." ("Mange de la merde" is a phrase used by some French people to express disgust about a person. The phrase sounds more vulgar in English than in French; it means "Eat shit.")

Sister Simeon's hearing was very good; she overheard my words and asked in a gruff voice, "What did you say?" I did not answer knowing my life was in danger. I didn't understand the full implications of my words, but I knew from her tone I had spoken badly. She had heard, and she punished me by tying me to her apron strings. (The Daughters of Wisdom sisters wore ancient grey uniforms with a long "bib" that had long apron strings.) I had to follow her around all day. When she sat at her desk, I had to sit by her on the floor; when she had recess duty, I had to stick by her, and could not play with my friends. I was untied from my "leash" only when she went to the bathroom in the inner sanctum of the convent. I would have preferred a beating with a strap, or a hitting-on-the-fingertips with a ruler.

Until the late 1960's, the teaching of English to French-speaking people in Northern Maine was done in what could be most charitably called a sledge hammer approach. Our French was belittled. We were told it was not true French – that it was inferior. The reality was different: Acadian French is partly ancient French which has not changed much due to isolation from France, Quebec, and other French-speaking peoples.

In the late 1960s and early 1970s, many Maine educators of French background assumed leadership positions in education and began to change the negative attitude about Acadian French. New teaching materials were developed, and our language was taught more fully. Also, the Acadian French of Northern Maine became increasingly seen as an asset, particularly by the Armed Forces, whose leaders saw military value in preserving French, and other languages spoken by Americans. Other educators came to recognize that knowing one's first language well – grammar, vocabulary, reading, and writing – makes it easier to learn another language. The experience of French-speaking people and educators in Northern Maine is a lesson writ large for those who would demean other people's languages, and those who would make English the official language of our country.

My mother tongue is imbedded in my flesh and bones. As a child I could not have explained why I resented being forced to learn English and why I spoke French in school whenever I could get away with it. I resisted learning to speak English until I went to college, where I finally became fluent. When I was a Peace Corps teacher in Thailand and taught English, my colleagues joked that my students spoke English with a French accent. I still speak English with a French lilt.

To belittle my language was to discredit my culture, my history, and my identity. Still, I learned much from Sister Simeon, and I hold no rancor in my heart for her. She taught me to respect my teachers and elders as my parents wanted her to do. And she taught me to speak English with a French-Acadian accent.

MOTHER AND SON

From my mother, Blanche, I learned to love books and reading and learning. I learned to treasure my French Acadian culture and language and I learned about God and life. Standing before her day, not taking herself too seriously, and with a steadying sense of humor, she got us ready for school, walked to church for Mass, read the Bible and the newspaper. And to close her day, she led the family in a rosary. This is how she raised her ten children and endured unrelenting fatigue and illness to age 92.

My mother's mother (Memére Corbin) was orphaned early, sent to live with an uncle far away, worked in an old people's home when very young, and married a lumberjack who spent winters in the Maine woods and returned home in spring drunk and broke. Through all this, Memére learned to value schooling. She scratched enough money together by cleaning homes, raising chickens, and selling eggs to see her children through high school – something like seeing children through college today, or more.

When things were trying for my mother, she talked about her father returning home after a winter's work in the woods with a barrel of unshelled peanuts and no money. I think she did this to remind herself that life was good in spite of difficulties. She remembered without resentment. She saw through her father's drunkenness and guilt the thoughtfulness of the unshelled peanuts, and she saw the good which resided in him side-by-side with his weaknesses. I learned to see this too.

There was no high school in Lille, so my mother, was sent to a boarding school run by the Daughters of Wisdom sisters in St. Agathe, Maine, some 30 miles away. She went by horse and buggy, came home only once or twice a year, at Christmas for sure and at Easter, maybe. My mother told me she never adjusted to being away from home; she was very lonely and cried most of her first year. The experience was so difficult – maybe traumatic – that she was never comfortable leaving her home in Lille. I think that experience, combined with her deep shyness, made her very reclusive; whenever my father suggested a short trip, ten or twenty miles from home, she had what today is called an anxiety attack. It strikes me that she did not pass her sense of loneliness or fear of leaving home to me; she never asked me if I was lonely or missed home during my four years of college in Nova Scotia, or when I was a Peace Corps Volunteer in Thailand. Maybe she felt a responsibility to pass on to me and her other children only her strengths, not her weaknesses. If so, she was wise in not wanting to raise copies of herself.

We didn't have much money, but unlike other families – many who had more money – we had some books, magazines, a dictionary, and a partial set of World Book of Knowledge in our home. My mother and her sister, Albertine, had pooled their pennies to buy the full set of the World Books of Knowledge when they were young, and had to break it up when they married and left home. When the Bangor Daily News and Time Magazine arrived in the mail, we split the newspaper in sections and read everything avidly. Reading was an integral part of our lives.

I think my earliest memory is of my mother reading to me a wonderful book illustrated with felted animals while sitting on her lap. I was no more than three or four years old, but I remember touching the fuzzy-wuzzy grey elephant and the tall giraffe and the striped zebra, loving the feel of them and learning new words. The book, her voice, and her warmth communicated love: love of books, love of reading, and love of me. I often fell asleep with that book, thinking of her and feeling her love.

My mother enjoyed a spirited conversation about religion and God, and didn't give an inch on her nun-inculcated principles, but she was open to learning, even from her children. Once when I was a teenager, she seemed to me overly worried about something which I thought unimportant, and I told her, "To worry shows lack of faith in God and in the Jesus of the Gospel." She listened and didn't comment. She probably felt good I had absorbed some knowledge of the Gospel.

After the church service on Sundays, we had to listen to my mother's interpretation of the homily. We joshed that we had two homilies, one in church and one at home. She was a conservative Catholic, but she didn't always agree with our conservative pastor; she respected him as a man of God, but understood he was human with all the frailties that meant. She didn't like it that our pastor didn't live the simple lifestyle he preached in his homilies, but she never said anything about his big black Buick, or Oldsmobile, or his vacation trips.

My mother was a good listener. One time – I think I was nine – it was my turn to go with my father and mother for a ride in our small 1947 Chevy coupe. This didn't happen often, with ten children vying for their turn. Waiting for my father in the car while he went into a hardware store, as he did whenever he was near one, my mother and I talked, or I should say I talked. I don't remember what we talked about, but I remember the closeness I felt with her as she listened to what I was saying. My mother couldn't spare much time for each child, but when I was with her I felt I was the most important person in the world.

HAVING TO KILL THE FAMILY CAT

I cried all the way to the river. I had never killed anything, but now I was going to kill the family cat. The
cat, more of a barn cat than a house pet, but almost
my pet, was very sick. I was the one who took care of the
cat, so my father asked me to kill it. I was in the 7th grade.
(We didn't use fancy words – to euthanize or to put to
sleep or to put away – we used "tuer" to kill. My father
said, "Il faut tuer le chat parcequ'il est malade", we must
kill the cat because it is sick.)

Killing animals to feed ourselves was a very personal matter in Lille. I had heard our pig squealing human-
like when being bled to death for its blood (to make blood
sausage), for its brain (to make boudin), and for its meat.
We raised chickens and pigs, and kept a cow for milk,
cream, and butter. Almost everyone kept animals. We
became attached to our animals, but eventually we had to
kill them for food.

Killing a pet was a different matter, and I had dif-
ficulty thinking about it. I didn't want to kill our cat, but
I had been told to do so. My father thought that learning
to kill animals was part of a boy's growing up. If he had
known my feelings about it, he might not have pushed so

hard. I was very upset, but didn't show it. Showing emotions in my family, particularly for a boy, was not something easily done. I kept delaying the whole matter. Finally, my father, impatient with my procrastination, told me the sick cat had to be put out of its misery and told me to kill it the next day.

Early morning before school started, I took an old burlap flour bag, a piece of twine, put the cat in the bag, and walked in the rain to drown the cat in the St. John River (the boundary between Maine and New Brunswick, Canada), about a quarter mile from our house. My father had suggested this way of killing the cat since he thought it was a humane way to do it. When I reached the river, I opened the bag, put a rock in it, tied it up, and threw it in the river. I hadn't chosen a heavy enough rock and the bag didn't go down immediately. It took what seemed an eternity, with the cat thrashing in the bag too long before the ordeal ended for the cat and me. I cried all the way back from the river to my home.

I can still feel the weight of the cat in the bag. Later, when I was asked to kill a chicken for a meal, I was adamant about not killing any chicken and my father relented. He placed the chicken's neck on a wood stump, cut it off with an axe, and let it loose to die, splattering blood all over the white snow in our yard. The saying, "running around like a chicken with its head cut off," has real meaning for me.

The memory of killing the family cat still stirs emotions in me. I'm not sure what lasting effect this has had on my life, if any. I don't hunt and fish, even though most people in Lille were hunters and fishers. Once, I was persuaded by a friend to hunt duck with him, but that was an aberration. Not only did we not kill any, we caused an international incident when a few of our bullets landed in someone's home across the St. John River in Canada.

No one was hurt, but the Mounties called the Maine State Police, who called the local police, who found us. We were not punished, but I think the incident further turned me off hunting. I've not hunted since. Maybe being forced to kill the family cat inhibited me from hunting, but I doubt it. From my very beginning, I was different from other Lille boys in not wanting to kill animals. Something deep inside me, coming from where I'm not sure, created that first impulse against killing anything.

Part II
High School Years, 1953 to 1957

LAWRENCE'S GENERAL STORE

I was too old to play with a child's toys and too young to work with my father. It was the summer of 1953. I was 14 years old and had graduated from eighth grade days earlier. It was an awkward time made more awkward by the growing hormonal disobedience in my groin – something I didn't understand; there was no talk of sex and hormones and girls and boys in my home or in my school.

Not knowing what to do with myself, I teased my younger sisters and got on my older sisters' nerves. My mother was ill (she was always sickly) and my older sisters, Noella and Priscille, had the thankless task of caring for me and our large family. I didn't like being told what to do or not do, and to have my older sisters doing the telling made it worse.

To get me out of the house, I think, Noella sent me to Lawrence's General Store to buy a jar of peanut butter. I loved peanut butter so I didn't fuss about running this errand. Years later, I tried to make peanut butter when I was a Peace Corps Volunteer in Thailand, but without good results. The mashed peanuts and peanut oil mixture didn't quite measure up, but I ate it anyway; "halfway" peanut butter was better than no peanut butter.

In minutes I was at Lawrence's store, which stood across the street from the school, the convent, and the church, which dominated the village. I stumbled into the store out of breath and placed my order with Lawrence. While he was getting the peanut butter and entering it on our account, I was horsing around with my friend, Ti Coune, and knocked down a display of workmen's boots all over the jam-packed entrance to the store. Lawrence was not pleased, and told me to restack the display. After I finished, he asked me to step inside his office. He knew my parents well – he was my dad's first cousin – and I feared a real dressing-down.

Lawrence told me I should be more careful, but he didn't scold me. Instead, he offered me a job in his store. He said he needed help to stack shelves, clean the store, pump gas and, if I did well, he would have me wait on customers. He offered to pay me 35 cents an hour. I said yes immediately. Thirty-five cents was a lot of money to me, and although I didn't see it then, being offered a regular paid job must have made me feel very grown up.

Lawrence's General Store was an institution in Lille – a kind of community center where serious matters were discussed, where people joked around and entertained each other. The store was the place where people gathered mornings, evenings, and on weekends to talk about the potato crop, who gave birth, who died, and to discuss town affairs, world affairs, and affairs no one was supposed to have.

The General Store had evolved into a community center not because it was in the physical center of Lille, but because it had been owned by community leaders for at least fifty years. Lawrence Parent was the town Postmaster, led the Church Choir, and had attended a Catholic seminary in Quebec City. He had bought the store from

Patrick Cyr, an influential and wealthy farmer, who had bought the store from Patrick Theriault, the first Acadian French to serve in the Maine Senate. Senator Theriault had worked hard to redress the traditional neglect of the St. John Valley Acadian French-speaking people, often discriminated against by the English-speaking population and the Maine State Legislature. In the 1950s, long after he died, he was still a source of pride.

My only earnings then came from serving Mass (I was an altar boy) and from babysitting. I got a dime for each Mass I served on weekdays from our pastor. Visiting priests would give me a little more, maybe 15 cents or a little less, maybe a nickel or maybe nothing. But it still beat attending Mass for no pay which my mother made me do anyway. I got no dime for serving Mass on Sundays because it was a day of obligation; I had to attend Mass under threat of mortal sin and eternal damnation. That didn't worry me much, because even then I didn't see God as vengeful and punitive; I saw God as a father who wouldn't hurt me. I attended Mass more to please my parents than to please God – they were a more immediate threat.

Working at Lawrence's was a practical education for me. I learned how to handle money, grind meat into hamburger, pump gas, make nice-looking – but not too large – ice cream cones, sell clothes, coax molasses from a huge cask, and keep the Coke machine full of Coke and the refrigerator full of beer. I learned the art of finding a rare machine screw to fix a plow, or rosin for my Uncle Alfred's fiddle, or harnesses for Aurele's horses, all in a warren of shelves, nooks, and crannies.

At the end of a late work day, when Lawrence was not around, I would close the store and bring the money from the cash register to my home. The sums were three or four hundred dollars – equivalent to much more today – a big responsibility which worried my mother. She worried too much; nothing happened in those days when people left their doors unlocked through the night.

I earned $155.00 at Lawrence's the summer of 1953. This was a lot of money, most of which I was made to save by my parents. I wanted to spend more of it, but my parents, having lost their savings in the bank failures of the 1930s, understood the need to save for the future. Those savings helped pay for my college education.

The store and the customers were a second family to me. We all knew each other and no one in the store hesitated to tease, to criticize, and to reprimand. Lawrence treated me like a son and taught me how to deal with the public. Working in the store made me more sure of myself. Lawrence, and occasionally a customer, would give me a compliment for a job well done, something I rarely got from my father when I later worked with him building houses.

Working at Lawrence's was more than a practical education: I learned about people, rich and poor and in the middle; I learned about the impact of illness on people's ability to buy food; I learned about different ways of looking at religion and God; I learned about alcoholism, mental illness, and more; I learned about life.

PATRICK O. AND SUNDAY MASS

On Sunday in Lille almost everyone attended Mass, and on Sunday in Lille, Patrick O. did not attend Mass. Everyone in Lille was Catholic, and the social pressure to be seen at Sunday Mass was heavy – almost oppressive. But Patrick O. did not bend to public opinion. He attended Mass Monday, Tuesday, Wednesday, Thursday, Friday, and Saturday, but not on Sunday. He started every day but Sunday by going to the 7:00 a.m. Mass in the big Acadian woodframe church with gold angels topping the spires, across from Lawrence's General Store.

After Mass, Patrick O. would come to Lawrence's where I worked. He was one of the regulars who came to the store daily to buy a few things, and to say a few words about the latest news with whoever was around. He was a quiet man who did not elaborate why he went to church every day but Sunday. Once, when asked, he said, "No one will tell me when to go to Mass."

Maybe he didn't want to be pestered by the collection basket. On weekdays there was no collection, but on Sundays the ushers passed the basket around two or three times: There was a regular collection for the parish, a special collection for the Bishop, or for the foreign missions, or for some other cause, and then there was the "pew" collection. I never understood the pew collection; you paid to build the church and you paid to sit in it.

I suspect that Patrick O.'s not attending Sunday Mass under threat of eternal damnation had nothing to do with Sunday collections, for he was not an uncharitable man. I think he knew that God does not care one whit when or how often he attended Mass or entered a church. In his guts, Patrick O. did not fear threats of priests and bishops and cardinals about eternal damnation because he knew those threats came from man and not from God. He knew that true worship comes from inside, not from outside.

I knew Patrick O. when he was old, or when he seemed old to the 14-year-old boy I was. I remember him talking about working on the railroad and cashing a railroad pension check at the store. Patrick O. was not well schooled, but he had achieved a sort of wisdom. He had visited faraway places and he had rubbed elbows with many kinds of people.

Patrick O. impressed me as a good, decent, and tolerant man. He was quiet and caused no waves, except in not attending Mass on Sunday. It pleases me today, given the piety of my home and the Catholic culture of my village, that I did not see Patrick O. as worse than anybody else. If anything, I was impressed by his disregard of a Church law and his dismissal of public opinion.

I THOUGHT I WAS IN
CATHOLIC SCHOOLS

I attended public schools until I went to private Universities, but these could easily have been taken for Catholic schools. The teachers at Notre Dame du Mont Carmel elementary school and those at my one-room high school (Lincoln High) were Catholic sisters who wore their ancient habits, to which a crucifix and rosary beads were visibly affixed. And Van Buren Boys High, where I completed my junior and senior years, was staffed mainly by Catholic priests who wore their cassocks in school. In every classroom a crucifix and other Catholic symbols hung on the walls. I thought my schools were Catholic.

Maybe it harmed no one that the schools were permeated with Catholic symbols and ideas; all the students in my elementary school and Lincoln High were Catholic. However, it was a different story at Van Buren Boys High, where there were students who were of other faiths, or no faith. I never thought about it then, but they must have felt left out, isolated, shut out.

Maybe those Catholic-faith-permeated public schools were not harmless; maybe they were harmful to the Catholic students and the few who were not Catholic.

Our Catholic teachers, directly and indirectly, taught that our Catholic religion was the only true religion. In doing so, they ignored, diminished, and downplayed the beliefs of millions of Americans, and sowed the seeds of narrow-mindedness, dogmatism, and bigotry in our young souls.

In fairness, these public schools grew out of the Catholic Schools established by Catholic parishes, priests and sisters in the early 20th century. And for many years after, when public funds partially supported the schools, sisters and priests worked for small stipends – much less than a regular teacher salary. There might have been no schooling in the early years had it not been for the initiative and hard work of the Catholic religious. Still, the religious symbols and ideas remained too long in the classrooms after they were fully supported with public funds.

In the mid-1950s, we were very much in the melting-pot-stage of our national life and, in French Northern Maine, that meant everyone had to melt into the French-Catholic pot.

FIXATED ON MONA

Mona was the most beautiful girl in my one-room high school. She sat on one side of the room with the girls and I sat on the other side with the boys. That's the way the classroom was set up by Sister St. Anne: girls to her right and boys to her left. I spent a lot of time trying to see Mona out of the corner of my eye, and fantasizing about her, as only teenage boys can do.

During my freshman year, I was too often bored and too often on teacher's nerves. One day, when the class was in disrepair, I did something – I've forgotten what – which must have cracked Sister's patience, for she got very upset and assigned me to a desk in the girl's section right behind Mona. She thought she was punishing me, but what a treat that was. I stopped disrupting the class, stopped annoying Sister St. Anne, and became a model student. I didn't want to lose my place near Mona.

Sitting behind Mona took my mind off misbehaving and studying. During the remainder of the school year, I lived in a teenage nirvana behind Mona. Too bad that I lived and acted my feelings for Mona only in fantasy-land; I was too shy in those 1950s days to date or hang out with girls. A few years later, in my senior year, Mona and I went to her prom, but that was my only date with Mona; she was – one could say – disinterested.

My performance in school was not affected by my teenage fixation on girls and sex. I learned easily, enjoyed school, and my grades were excellent. Where my head and my heart and my emotions wandered made no difference academically or in any other way I can tell.

SOCIALLY CHALLENGED AT BOYS HIGH

I was apprehensive about too many things: my looks, my clothes, my acne, girls, sex, masturbation – it was supposed to do bad things to you – fitting in with a new group, and finding my way around a new and much larger school in a strange town. At Lincoln High, I could not get lost for it had only one room and one teacher but, at Van Buren Boys High, there was a social gap for me to close, and I magnified it way out of proportion to reality. Later in life, I learned that how I feel does not always correspond to reality . . . but that was much later. At fifteen, I thought it did.

I did not experience a significant intellectual break from Lincoln High to Boys High. I was better prepared than I realized for the more varied subject matter and the slightly more intellectual atmosphere. I thrived academically, consistently earned high grades, and was one of two salutatorians of my graduating class. My mother believed there should have been only one salutatorian and I should have been the one; she thought the teachers and administrators of Van Buren Boys High favored students from Van Buren. I don't know if her gut feelings were right, but I didn't dwell on that issue. Special honors and recognition didn't mean much to me then, and don't mean much to me now.

The way I remember it, I grew very little socially at Boys High. I suppose I became more comfortable in some social settings but, who knows. It's hard to remember exactly what was happening to me for I did not have the capacity to see myself objectively.

I participated in class discussions very little, and did so mainly to draw attention to myself in a funny way. Once, my English teacher had a spirited conversation going among the students about sports, and everyone was shouting, "I'm a Red Sox fan, I'm a Dodger fan, I'm a Yankee fan." When I piped up, "I'm an electric fan," everybody burst out laughing. That was the last thing they had expected from me.

I was a transfer student intruding in an established classroom social situation; I knew only a handful of students who had matriculated from Lincoln High, and I knew no teachers. When a priest/teacher who was too "touchy-feely" came around from time to time to massage my neck and shoulders, I was too naive to pick up on what everyone else knew...that he was gay. Nothing happened, but it was embarrassing to learn more than a year later that everyone but me had known he was gay.

As the name Boys High implies, there were no girls in the classroom to talk with and fantasize about. At Lincoln High I was surrounded by girls and had developed a kind of rapport with a few. At Van Buren, I regressed in my relationships with girls because there were none in the school, and meeting some after school in extracurricular activities was impossible because my bus to Lille left immediately after the end of classes.

When a teacher complimented me on a good paper or my grades, there was always a smart ass in class who would say, "There's nothing else to do in Lille but study, that's why he gets good grades." I resented this quietly. They couldn't have known I didn't study much, and worked many hours after school and on weekends at Lawrence's General Store.

I never fully became part of the class or any in-group. Almost all the students had known each other practically from birth or at least from kindergarten, and they lived in cliques. I hung around with a few other nerdy types; I suppose you could say we were a clique too. During lunch breaks, we played handball and talked about what we thought were important matters. We looked down on the in-crowd – a crowd we would have eagerly joined had they welcomed us.

When I attended my 20th high school reunion, I discovered that the nice, kind, and thoughtful students were still nice, kind, and thoughtful, and that the inconsiderate, boorish, and cliquish students were still inconsiderate, boorish, and cliquish. One thing I particularly enjoyed about the reunion was the pleasant discovery that many of the less popular girls from Girls' High had matured into beautiful women, and many had married nerds who had become quite successful.

FORTUNA AND PEPÉRE CORBIN AND BINGE DRINKING

When I opened Lawrence's store around seven in the morning, Fortuna was often waiting to buy a beer – not just any beer, but a big quart-sized bottle of Schmidt beer. He had waited for the store to open and he was ready for his first beer of the day. Fortuna was an alcoholic; he drank until the bottle was empty, then drank another and another until his money ran out. One night on my way home from the store, I found him drunk in the gutter.

My Pepére (Acadian French for grandfather) Corbin, drank the same way Fortuna did – as long as his liquor and his money held out or until he passed out. Memére Corbin fought his drinking every way she could. If she found liquor in the house, she emptied it into the kitchen sink. I saw her do that once, and remember Pepére being in tears over it. Many years later, after Memére died, and Pepére was in an "old people's" home in St-Basile, Uncle Cyr (Pepére's son) would sneak a bottle of liquor to his room and they would empty it in themselves.

My mother was deathly afraid of alcohol, because she knew firsthand from her family the awful effects it could have. Her father worked winters in the logging camps of Maine, received most of his earnings in one lump sum, and returned home in late spring already drunk – with little money left for his family.

Fortuna and Pepére Corbin learned to drink during prohibition when it was illegal to have or drink any kind of alcohol. Pepére smuggled liquor from Canada over the iced up St. John River or in his canoe during summer, carried it to his favorite hangout and drank it all in one sitting so no officer could find it and fine him. That's how he learned binge drinking.

When I was growing up, there was no liquor in my home, mainly because of my mother's fear that if we touched alcohol we would become alcoholics. I drank a few beers once to celebrate the end of potato picking season, felt woozy, and didn't like that feeling. In college, I only drank a few beers during the entire four years. Today I enjoy beer and wine, but I can take it or leave it. My wife, Rolande, and I offered our teenage children a bottle of beer or a glass of wine from time to time and often they declined. I know some of our four children experimented with liquor at University, and probably drank too much occasionally, but none abuse alcohol today, and some don't drink it at all.

MY FATHER'S SHEETROCK TRICK

I learned from my father to hit a nail on the head, to saw a board in a straight line, and to visualize a house from a hole in the ground. I learned that taking the first step, not quite knowing the next, was the way to tackle any project, big or small, simple or complicated. Standing by the hole that would be the cellar to a house while chewing over his next move, my father would say, "If we're going to build this house, we have to start."

My father, Noel, was a master carpenter who built homes. A person who wanted a home would call on him with a rough idea, some pictures, and magazine plans. If my father took the job, he would develop architectural plans – he was a self-taught draftsman – hire laborers, electricians, and plumbers, and supervise all aspects of the construction.

In 1950s rural Maine, and maybe still today, home construction was not a matter of specialized crews: my father and a few workers laid out the footprint of the house, supervised the excavation, built the foundation, framed, roofed, shingled, dry-walled, floored, wallpapered, painted, and did the cabinetry. When my brothers and I were old enough to work with him, we had to quickly learn a great variety of skills.

My father had a reputation as a hard man to work for and he deserved it. He did not believe in compliments: "No need for a compliment if it's done right, that's the way it should be." No matter how near-perfect the cut, or how tight the joint, he would find something to critique, and the work would have to be done over. He was equally hard on himself; he would redo his work on his time when it did not meet his standards.

My father had another side to him – a mischievous and fun side. He loved to challenge his workers; he especially enjoyed playing the "sheetrock closet trick" on them. Almost every house we built had a closet with a small door – 2 feet 6 inches wide by 6 feet 8 inches tall. He would ask one or two of his workers to install a 4 feet by 8 feet panel of sheetrock or gypsum in the closet without cutting the panel – an impossible task since the doorway would not allow that size panel through. And there could be no joint in the sheetrock.

He would say, "it should take about fifteen minutes or so to do this job." They would try every conceivable way to get the 4 feet by 8 feet panel in the closet, with no success.

After a while, my father would nonchalantly amble into the room and ask, "How are you doing?"

They would shake their heads in frustration, "this is an impossible task." My father would eat his lunch quickly, go in the room when no one was looking, and install the panel in very little time, showing no joints. Here's how he did this: He cut the back of the panel with his utility knife, being careful not to perforate the panel's front paper cover. Then he carefully folded the panel in half, making it small enough to pass in the door opening. Once the panel was inside the closet, he unfolded it and nailed it into place. Voila! No joint! Then my father would show off his work to the workers. They were incredulous. "How did you do this?" He would not tell them his secret right away . . . maybe he would do so at the end of the job.

My father also had a generous and humane spirit. He led volunteers in building an addition to our elementary school and in constructing a new firehouse; he designed and helped to rebuild our neighbor's burned-out house. One day, while working in Madawaska, he was asked by a widow if he would teach carpentry to her young son, Albert. She was afraid he would grow up with no skills and get in needless trouble along the way. My father taught Albert every aspect of his trade; Albert slept in our home many nights.

Albert grew into a master carpenter, became a foreman, and later an executive of a large construction company in Chicago. It's in Albert that my father's reputation for high standards in home construction lives on. I chose another career. My father's honesty and integrity, his quest for perfection, his ability to see whole, at the outset, a complicated project, and always giving more than what was asked of him, affect my life daily.

SPIRITUALITY IN A HAMMOCK

On a beautiful Sunday afternoon when I was 15 or 16, I was swaying lazily in a hammock in the shade of trees planted by my father years earlier, feeling dejected and a little sorry for myself. I had missed my ride to Birch Point Beach at Long Lake, Lawrence's General Store (the village social center) was closed, and my parents were visiting Mon Oncle (Uncle) Alfred and Tante (Aunt) Louise on their farm a few miles away. Many people had gone to the beach, others were out for a Sunday drive or were taking an afternoon nap. I was alone at home and felt alone in Lille and in the whole world. Lille was quiet like an abandoned cemetery.

The sky was a perfect light blue dotted with small grayish clouds, like the picture of the imagined soul dotted with "sin spots" in Sr. Sister Simeon's classroom. The rapidly flowing St. John River, separating Maine from Canada, glistened in the sunlight about 2,000 feet to my right, and to my left the white blossoms of potato plants drew my eyes to the hills rimming the St. John Valley. A slight breeze carried to me the sweet aroma of the blossoms and the fragrance of our lilac tree. And as the hammock swung slowly, I fingered the grass, too long for a lawn and too short for a hayfield.

This bucolic and tranquil scenery was unremarkable to me. What was remarkable that day was a growing feeling that I was part of this land in a way I had never experienced. My body, mind, and spirit seemed intimately connected, suffused, and intermingled with everything: the hammock, the grass, the trees, the river, the blossoms, the sky, and the cows nearby. Instead of observing, I was part of my surroundings, and peace flowed through me and around me.

I was dejected no more and did not feel sorry for myself. I felt happy in a way that had nothing to do with things or with a girlfriend I wanted or with a car I wished for. The peacefulness and sense of oneness with my surroundings and beyond were exhilarating, calming, reassuring.

At the time I didn't see this profound experience on a beautiful Sunday afternoon as a hint of the deeper and more personal relationship I could have with God. Later, I recognized it as such and tried to recapture this experience, but without much success. My early life was full of religion, but empty of a personal relationship with God.

Growing up Catholic in my family included more than the usual baptism, first communion, Sunday Mass, and meatless Fridays. It meant family Rosary most evenings, and Eucharistic Adoration at 2:00 p.m. Sundays; it meant special services to honor our Holy Mother Mary during the month of May, and no sweets during four weeks of Advent and forty days of Lent. I heard much about how participation in these religious practices would make me a good Catholic, but not much about building a personal relationship with God.

I shouldn't be surprised. It was not the purpose of these religious practices to create a personal experience of God. Their purpose was to train me to obey the priest, to follow the rules of the Church, and to shape me into a good Catholic – one submissive to the Church. The objective was not against building a personal and unique relationship with God, it was simply not geared to that idea.

I remember my early religious practices with nostalgia, but do not adhere to most of them today. I don't fully regret the religious disciplines imposed on me by my parents and my culture; they provided a framework for my life which served me well for a long time. But I rue the years those practices and disciplines stood in the way of establishing a more mature spirituality and a more adult relationship with God.

Part III
Saint Francis Xavier University, 1957 to 1961

THE ROAD TO COLLEGE

When I was young, it was not given I would go to college. In the fifties of rural Northern Maine, only children of professionals – doctors, lawyers, dentists – and of very successful farmers and merchants, went to college.

My mother, Blanche, a high school graduate with a few teacher training courses, had been a teacher in a one-room school during the Depression of the 1930s, and my father was a master carpenter with about four years of school. My parents placed a strong emphasis on learning, and thought it would be a major accomplishment to get their ten children through high school.

One day, out of the blue, Father Omer, Principal of Van Buren Boys High School, got a hold of my father, Noel, and asked to talk with him. My father must have wondered what he wanted. He probably thought Father Omer wanted to talk about a carpentry project: my six older brothers and sisters who had matriculated to Van Buren High School were excellent students – near the top of their class – and he knew none were in academic trouble.

My father took off from building a house to meet

with Father Omer, prepared to discuss a carpentry project, and maybe some work for him. But that's not what Father Omer wanted to talk about; he wanted to talk about my older brother, Richard. He told my father, "Richard is intelligent, hard-working, and talented; he should go to college." Father Omer's words made a big impression on my father. To have a priest who was also a principal, tell him that Richard should go to college was very persuasive. Catholic priests in those days were highly influential, and moved among community leaders – not in the lower social circle of my parents.

My father could not see how to pay for college on a carpenter's salary, given his large family. Besides, he knew that Richard was already a skilled carpenter, and he would have been pleased to see him follow in his footsteps. But he knew, too, that carpentry is physically demanding and not always financially secure. Also, the idea of one of his sons being an engineer – Father Omer had mentioned this – played to his ego. The problem was money: there were no federal loans and grants for college students in those days; college expenses were the sole responsibility of the parents and the student. The idea of paying for college must have seemed overwhelming, if not impossible.

My father thanked Father Omer, and said he too believed Richard could do well in college, and that he would like Richard to attend, but he didn't have the money. Father Omer was insistent and persistent; he said, "It would be unfortunate if Richard did not go to college; it would be a loss to himself, his future family and his country." He detailed the typical cost of college, and showed my father how Richard's summer earnings, part-time work in college, and some financial help, could make college feasible.

When my father returned home after a long, ten-hour work-day, he and my mother discussed his conversation with Father Omer. I didn't learn the details until some years later, but I knew my parents had told Richard that if he wanted to go to college, they would try to help him. They put no pressure on him; the decision was completely his. My mother and father never tried to influence us toward this or that career or occupation. When we were eighteen, we were adults, and it was assumed we could and would make those important decisions.

Richard went to St. Francis Xavier University in Nova Scotia, and majored in Chemical Engineering. Two years later I followed him and majored in Economics. My brother Paul enrolled at the University of Connecticut using the G.I. Bill, and most of my brothers and sisters graduated from college. Three earned graduate degrees.

Father Omer changed the thinking of my family. When he reached out to my father and mother about college for Richard, he could not have predicted the large impact this would have on Richard's life, on mine, and on that of my brothers and sisters. We had not thought a college education possible until he planted that seed of hope in our family. His initiative and my parent's generous response helped shape my life, and created a legacy which lives in my children and grandchildren, and all to come.

ROADS NOT TAKEN

When I was an altar boy, I considered being a priest. My parents had cousins who were priests, nuns, and brothers, and when I was fifteen, my sister, Emelda, started studying to become a Daughter of Wisdom Sister. She's still a Sister today. The idea of being a priest attracted me until I reached puberty, when girls attracted me much more. Why the Catholic Church demands celibate priests only, and why women are not ordained to the priesthood eludes me. This, and other more theological factors, keep me distant from the Church today.

When I was sixteen, I heard of the big money a carpenter could make in Alaska and I wanted to be a carpenter in Alaska. During my sophomore year in college, I decided to be a history teacher; at the beginning of my junior year, I planned to be an economist; and at the end of my junior year, I wanted to be a political scientist. I graduated with a Bachelor's degree in Economics and took many courses in political science.

Some people are born with a gene or a push from their parents for a specific career: they know when very young they're going to be a farmer or a doctor or a teacher or a carpenter or a business person. I didn't know, but not knowing was liberating. It freed me to choose whatever subjects interested me at the moment, and it made of my college studies an interesting mishmash of courses.

Going to college was my decision; my parents did not have a career in mind for me, nor did I. Their only expectation – one they didn't have to express – was that I would study hard, learn much, and get the best grades I was capable of. They had imbued me with a love of learning for the sake of learning, not for any career goal.

In my home we had a small number of books, a few magazines and the Bangor Daily News; my mother read everything, and my father read magazines and the newspaper. By their example and attitude, my parents communicated the importance of reading and learning, but they never told me doing so would get me a better paying job or a bigger career. I loved learning and I was curious about everything; I spent much time in the library reading books that had nothing to do with my courses. I was eager to learn history and not eager to learn Latin, a required course. I thought studying a dead language was a stupid way to learn another language; I'd already learned English from my Acadian French teacher without learning Latin.

I took easily to Thomistic philosophy and the logic of first premises and syllogisms. I studied physics to test myself and found out I was good at analyzing the problems, but not so good at the math needed to solve those problems. I worked hard at math, and when I was the only student to walk in a blinding blizzard to my math classroom, my professor, Father M., said, "Let's get on with the class; you're probably the only student who's been paying attention all year anyway."

I excelled in economics and political science. In a tough course on micro-economics, I discovered a technical error in our textbook, and brought it to the attention of Prof. William, who confirmed the error and complimented me on finding it. I admired two political science professors, John and Walter, who stimulated my interest in politics. John became a highly respected member of the Canadian Parliament.

My days in college didn't fix me on a career, but they confirmed my love of learning, excited my curiosity in politics, economics, philosophy, and theology, and opened my eyes to the world outside North America.

POKER

When I arrived at St. Francis Xavier University, I found myself living with fourteen other guys in one large room in the basement of Mockler Hall. This was terrific; it was almost like living at home with my nine brothers and sisters. In this big room, filled with seven bunk beds and one cot, lived a polyglot mix of people from Canada, Northeastern U.S., and from the island country of St. Lucia in the Caribbean. We were together in this big basement room because it was the least expensive place to stay - none of us had much money.

One thing I did early on was to organize a poker game. I had learned poker in Lille, played with older men who knew the game well, and I was fairly good at it. There wasn't much to do in Lille - no movie house, no organized sports - and we played poker to entertain each other. My parents didn't like poker, and rarely played any card games, but the stakes were low and I lost no money doing so.

During the first semester of my freshman year, I studied almost all the time. I wasn't confident of my ability to do college work, and wanted to make sure I would get passing grades or better. That's been the formula of my life: if unsure of success with a project, work harder than anybody else. Maybe it would have been better to work less and to play more; I might have done just as well. Poker was my recreation during the first semester of my freshman year for a few hours a week.

We had anywhere from four to six or seven players playing nickel-and-dime games. No one lost much; the wins and losses pretty much evened out. Anyway, no one could afford to lose; we were playing with our lunch money.

We played poker almost every weekend for three or four hours during the first semester, and started up again after Christmas. A basement roommate (I'll call him Bill) who had not played the first semester joined our first game of the second semester. He played well, and won many hands, resulting in losses for me and the other players. The next game, Bill joined us, and again he did very well. I was getting a little concerned about my losses, even though it was less than those of the other players.

The next time we played, Bill suggested a new game called Red Dog, which allowed the jackpot to build. He also suggested we play for higher stakes – dimes and quarters instead of nickels and dimes. We agreed with Bill, played Red Dog, and the jackpot grew to nearly fifty dollars – a huge sum of money for poor college students in the late 1950s. I became very apprehensive about the game and the amount of money I had in it, yet stayed in to recoup my losses. I had confidence in my ability to play with as much or more skill than anyone else at the table. Still, I was very wary of Bill; I knew he was not playing better than I, yet he was winning more. I watched him like a hawk, and when he dropped a card on the floor under the table and bent down to retrieve it, I saw him switch cards. He was cheating.

I had never knowingly played with someone who cheated and didn't know how to handle it. I immediately left the game with no money for my meals, and so did the other players – we were all hurting for money. I told the other players privately that I had seen Bill cheating. We talked about approaching Bill, but decided it would be my word against his, plus we also wanted to maintain peace in our basement room where we all lived cheek-by-jowl. Bill's cheating changed the climate of the room; we kept our valuables under lock and key, and we never played poker again.

REVEREND R. SAYS I CHEATED

I knew I had done well on a midterm exam in the "Survey of English Literature" course; I had taken copious notes, had memorized them completely, and had anticipated all the questions. Still, I was surprised when the exam papers were handed out by Rev. R. to see a perfect score on the front page. I had not expected a perfect score, but my grades had always been good and I had hoped to do well.

Rev. R. prefaced his lecture that morning with a scolding to the class: he was disappointed that the students had done very poorly on the exam; he said there had been only one perfect score, and that it was so far above the others that surely the student must have cheated to get it. He did not name me, but he said "the cheat knows who he is."

I was dumbfounded, incredulous, speechless. My feelings had changed instantly from happiness with a perfect score to sadness at being called a cheat.

I had never cheated in any classroom. Honesty in word and deed topped the list of virtues in my home, and any act or word deviating from the highest standard was punished. As a child, I had stolen a cucumber from a neighbor's garden, and my parents had taught me a lesson

I've never forgotten. They made me get a cucumber from our garden and bring it to the neighbor as restitution. My embarrassment was compounded when my cousin, Velma, who was baby-sitting, met me at the door; I had to tell her what I was doing there with a cucumber. That's how dishonesty was handled in my home.

My sadness quickly turned to anger, then to embarrassment. No one in the theater-style classroom had seen my exam papers, and I quickly hid them in my note-book. I could not concentrate on Rev. R.'s lecture that morning. I knew I should say something to Rev. R.; I knew I should confront him with his gross and unjust accusation, but I was too shy and unsure of myself.

In my family, we were as shy and timid as we were honest and hardworking. We were intelligent, but most of us shone mainly on paper, and not in our involvement in class and after-school activities. I opted out of many potentially valuable school experiences because of shyness. When I ran for the South Bend City Council many years later, shyness was the first hurdle I had to overcome.

I was too insecure to talk with Rev. R. about his unjust accusation, and he was too feckless and insensitive to talk with me. Subsequently, my heart left his course, and my final grade was barely passing. He probably thought my silence about his accusation and my final grade proved my guilt. I'm still appalled that Rev. R. would accuse me of cheating without proof and without discussing it with me. Maybe he was unsure of his ability; maybe he couldn't have gotten a perfect score on an exam except by cheating. These questions – possibly unfair questions – more than 40 years later reveal the depth of my unresolved feelings.

MY ROOMMATE CARL OF GRENADA

I'm listening to steel band music of St. George's, Grenada in South Bend, Indiana, and remembering Carl. Carl was my roommate in my senior year at St. Francis Xavier University. He had a large influence on me, but he doesn't know it because I never told him . . . maybe I didn't fully realize that until now.

Carl and I were very different. Carl was self-confident, I was not; he was outgoing and gregarious, I was shy and reserved; he had many friends, I had a few; he came from a very small country, I came from a very large country. But the real difference between us was our world view. Carl had a large world view and I had a narrow world view.

I was too proud of my country and too quick to defend it, as someone tends to do when not accepted as a full citizen in one's country. French-speaking persons of long standing in Northern Maine were not always accepted as full citizens. Carl didn't take easily to my narrow view and debunked many of my chauvinistic notions. He was my passport to a broader world.

I met Carl in my freshman year when he visited his friends from St. Lucia in our large Mockler Hall basement room. Fifteen students lived in the big room, including two from St. Lucia, Pat, and Bob. Through them and Carl, I met students from many other countries – including India, Kenya, Nigeria, Ghana, Trinidad, Latin America, Bangladesh, Iraq, and Switzerland. I socialized with many of these students, particularly during school breaks when, being far from home, we stayed on campus.

I was very lucky to have chosen St. Francis Xavier University. Today, it is de rigueur, obligatory for a University to be seen as diverse and worldly. In 1957, St Francis Xavier was that and still is today. St. Francis Xavier, with a student body of about one thousand students, located in small Antigonish, Nova Scotia (less than six thousand people then), had an international flavor absent from many larger universities and towns. There were students from most Canadian provinces, many from the northeastern United States, and some representing another 20 countries or so. I had my first personal exposure to a world very different from my world of French-speaking Lille, Maine, through Carl and his friends, and through the international spirit of St. Francis Xavier University.

After graduation in 1961, our paths diverged and we lost track of each other. Carl pursued a graduate degree and became a Canadian citizen. I joined Peace Corps, went to Thailand, did graduate work at the University of Notre Dame, and became involved in South Bend, Indiana politics. After leaving the South Bend Mayor position in 1989, I directed Peace Corps in Grenada, and asked my barber if he knew Carl's family. He did and said they lived in a yellow house a few blocks away. I walked to the yellow house, knocked on the door, and a very old man answered. I introduced myself as Carl's former roommate at St. Francis Xavier University, and asked if he was Carl's father: "Yes, I'm Carl's father."

"Where's Carl these days?"

"He lives in Ottawa, but he's here vacationing. He's visiting friends and should be home in a few hours." Later that day, Carl and I got reacquainted, introduced our wives to each other, and talked about the two things we always had in common; our love of politics and economics.

LIGHTS OUT AT 11:00 P.M.

It always happened at a bad time – in the middle of writing a paper due next day, or when doing a tough math assignment, or while listening to a favorite song or during a lively argument with friends. The hall rector would cut the power to student rooms, killing all light bulbs and neutering all electric outlets, leaving us in the dark. At St. Francis Xavier University there was a curfew and lights-out policy from 11:00 p.m. to 6:00 a.m., and the hall rector made the rounds to make sure we were in our rooms. This was the rule when I was a student from 1957 to 1961.

Lights out and curfew in college didn't make sense to me. Why would young adults preparing for a career be treated as children? My parents had long ago stopped asking me to turn off the lights in my room late at night. Turning off the power to students' rooms was more about controlling than about protecting; it was an opportunity for "small" people who had a little power to use it on students, who had even less power.

During my freshman year in Mockler Hall I studied and read in the bathroom under dim lights. During my sophomore year in Augustine Hall I purchased a long extension cord, which I plugged into the bathroom outlets, blacked out my room windows, and studied and talked with my friends to my heart's content after 11:00 p.m. During my junior year, sick of this lights-out policy, I lived off campus.

I soon got tired of walking to classes and moved back on campus for my senior year. I brought my long extension cord to Chisolm Hall with me. After the lights were turned off and room check was completed, I taped black paper to the windows, pulled the shades, and continued studying and listening to music. This went on for some time until Rev. C. B., a top university official, saw dim light emanating from a student's room. He entered Chisolm Hall, walked up to the second level, and found an extension cord leading from the bathroom to my room.

Suddenly, my roommate and I were in the dark. Rev. C. B. had unplugged the extension cord and was following it to my room as I was leaving to check the problem. That was the end of my after-lights-out studying. This happened during the last months of my senior year, and my only punishment was losing my extension cord. After that, I sneaked out of my room almost every night and went to the nearby Wagon Wheel student hangout, where I studied and had my favorite treat of milk and cinnamon rolls.

I didn't give up on the lights-out-and-curfew practice. I wrote a long letter to the University Administration and an article for the college newspaper, The Xaverian, titled: "Reasons for All Night Lights." Here's some of what I said: "Sleep . . . is essential for good health, but too much of a good thing can be bad . . . a person's eagerness and dedication for something determines the amount of sleep a person needs . . . and if you treat college students as children, they will act as children."

ARM-WRESTLING

When I got tired of studying in the library or bored in the dormitory, I suggested arm-wrestling. I was good at arm-wrestling, despite my slight physique. Maybe it was all the hammering and sawing while building homes with my father, or maybe it was my daily regime of pushups and chin-ups. More likely, it was technique and psychology, not physical strength that made me arm-wrestling "champ" of my floor. I enjoyed taking on bigger guys in a way I could best them physically, and did so at every opportunity.

To intimidate my opponents, I approached arm-wrestling matches projecting confidence. First, I took on a guy my size and said: "I will win, you have absolutely no chance to win," and as soon as we were in position and the call was made to start, I immediately smacked his arm on the table, not even giving him a chance to think winning. This set the stage for bigger challengers.

At some point, a much taller and stronger student – maybe 6' and 200 lbs. to my 5'8" and 145 lbs. – would challenge me. In his eyes I was a little runt he could crush. A tall person may not realize that, in arm-wrestling, the person with shorter forearms has a leverage advantage which can negate greater strength. Also, a strong person accustomed to winning physical contests can be overconfident. My strategy consciously played to that overconfidence.

A crowd would usually gather and root for me because "I'm the underdog – I'm their David to Goliath." Displaying great confidence, I would grab my opponent's hand – a hand twice the size of mine (maybe I'm exaggerating here) – look him straight in the eye, and tell him, "You have no greater chance of winning this match than a snowball's chance in hell; you will definitely lose."

When the call was made to start, I made no move: I held a dead center position with all my strength. Then, to make my challenger think he had a chance of winning and to feed his overconfidence, I let my wrist (not my arm) bend backward to about 60 degrees. That allowed me to rest my arm because my opponent's pressure was directly on my wrist. After he had expended much energy in this position and was getting tired, I brought my wrist up and put tremendous downward pressure on him, chattering throughout, "You have a weak wrist and arm, there's no way you can win this contest, you better give up before you hurt yourself," and on and on. Then in a quick move, I brought his arm down to three or four inches from the table where he made a strong last-ditch effort, got very tired, and gave up, letting the back of his hand hit the table hard.

No one else came forward to challenge me – a good thing, for my arm was completely worn out.

To Help People in a Poor Country

Graduation was only months away and I wanted to go help people in a poor country far from home. In 1961, the idea of a one- or two-year volunteer stint after college was not popular; it was almost radical. Most college graduates got a job or were drafted into the army or went to graduate school. Some of my friends thought that to volunteer would be a waste of time – better to get a job, earn money, buy a car, get married. Today, to volunteer after college at home or abroad is popular with many college students.

For me, volunteering to help people in a poor country far from home seemed a natural thing to do. If it was not in my genes, it was certainly in my surroundings. The year 1961 was only 16 years removed from the end of World War II; I had heard many stories about battles and poverty in the South Pacific islands from Uncle Roland and Uncle Cyr, and from other war veterans.

Perhaps more inspiring were the conversations in my home about the work of my mother's two missionary cousins: Frere Christophe was a Catholic Brother in Cameroon, and Sister Abela was a missionary in Madagascar. When they came home every five years or so, they had a meal with us and talked about their work among the poor in these far-off exotic places. But even more influential in my decision to volunteer a few years in a developing country were the international spirit of St. Francis Xavier University and the friends I made there – friends from Africa, Latin America, the Caribbean, and Asia.

When President John F. Kennedy, in his first inaugural address on January 20, 1961, challenged Americans, "Ask not what your country can do for you, ask what you can do for your country," I took it personally. When he promised to establish the Peace Corps to recruit, train, and send volunteers to poor countries around the world, I was ready to sign up.

My motivation was probably not completely altruistic; I wanted to help but I also wanted adventure – a different kind of adventure. Military service, a given for me as it was for most able-bodied American men in the 1960s (at least for those in my socioeconomic situation), would have to wait. I had no qualms about serving my country in the military, and felt it was my responsibility. My two brothers, Paul and Richard, had been drafted into the Army, and I had many relatives who had served in World War II; I was too imbued with the culture of military duty to even think of avoiding military service.

For now, I wanted only to defer being drafted in the Army for the adventure of helping people in a poor country far away.

PEACE CORPS?
CHRISTIAN BROTHERS? SOLDIER?

Wanting to help poor people overseas was one thing, finding a program to do so was another. I had heard about the need for teachers in a high school run by Christian Brothers in Odo, Nigeria, and talk of the Peace Corps had percolated during John F. Kennedy's campaign for president and after his inauguration. I was inspired by President Kennedy's Peace Corps idea and wanted to be part of it, but I didn't know when it would be established, and could not wait very long. Still, I wrote to President Kennedy in February 1961, "If you are going to establish the Peace Corps, I would like to serve in it."

Acting much more quickly than I had anticipated, President Kennedy, on March 1, 1961, created the Peace Corps. Immediately, I wrote to Sargent Shriver, Peace Corps Director, and volunteered. However, I was not optimistic about serving in the Peace Corps, because I believed it would take time to get this federal program functioning. Furthermore, even if the organization was established quickly, the publicity about the tens of thousands who wanted to join, and the high standards expected of volunteers, were daunting. By March 1, 1961, more than 30,000 people had indicated interest in joining the Peace Corps.

As backup plan I wrote to Brother Maurice, a Christian Brother in Toronto, volunteering to teach in one of their schools in Nigeria. I got an immediate response of interest in my services, and my letter was forwarded to Brother Broderick in London, who was on his way to Nigeria. In those days, there was no e-mail or fax machines or practical international telephone communications, so the back-and-forth of letters concerning credentials and references took much time. By graduation on May 17, I did not have a definitive response from the Christian Brothers, nor had I heard from the Peace Corps.

About a week after graduation, I received my first news from the Peace Corps in a letter from Sargent Shriver, telling me I had made the first cut from the thousands who had applied, and inviting me to take the Peace Corps Entrance Examination on May 27 at the Post Office in Caribou, Maine. Sargent Shriver's letter was immediately followed by a letter from President Kennedy congratulating me "for being among the first to volunteer for the Peace Corps."

Getting letters from the President and his brother-in-law was heady stuff, and I tried not to get too excited and puffed up about it – not something my family would have tolerated anyway. Although volunteering to serve abroad and not seeking a paying job was far from the norm in those times, I sensed a real approval from my parents. They must have felt that volunteering for the Peace Corps was a worthy thing to do. But they didn't comment much on my plans; they shied away from unduly influencing my major life decisions.

The summer after my graduation, I returned to my old jobs – carpentry work with my father and part-time work at Lawrence Parent's General Store in Lille – not knowing what I would end up doing. I no longer held a deferment from military service and I expected to be drafted shortly. Serving in the Armed Forces was one job I didn't have to apply for.

DRAFT BOARD CLERK VS. ME

In Aroostook County, Maine, the clerk of Local Draft Board #2 had awesome power over me. Draft boards were made up of volunteers from the area, but the clerk had much discretion in wielding the power of the Board; it was the clerk who had the power to decide my immediate future, not the faceless board members.

The clerk wore the now funny-looking, but then-stylish glasses of the late 1950s on the end of her pointed nose. She had a pursed mouth with startup wrinkles radiating upward, downward, and sideways. She exuded a strict professional demeanor which made her seem cold and uncaring. She may have been warm and considerate, but that's not how I remember her.

The first thing I had to do after returning from Antigonish, Nova Scotia to Lille in May 1961 with a college degree in my back pocket was to visit the draft board clerk in Caribou. I had to report my change of status from college student to carpenter's helper.

It was to the clerk I had earlier addressed my requests to defer my military obligation for college. She had approved those requests, but I felt she had done so reluctantly. I assumed, rightly or wrongly, that she thought

I was trying to evade the draft, but I only wanted to go to college. I reported my change of status and started the waiting game. What would I be? Peace Corps Volunteer? Christian Brother Volunteer? Soldier?

The summer of 1961 was not just about waiting and working. Evenings and weekends I went to dances, lake beaches, checked out the girls, and dated Rolande – a smart and beautiful woman I married a few years later. It was a carefree summer with no real worries. By fall, I'd be adventuring somewhere. Nevertheless, it seemed a long wait and I was getting impatient.

The first good news arrived on August 8 in a letter from the Christian Brothers offering me a teaching position at St. Joseph's College in Odo, Nigeria. I immediately accepted their offer and petitioned the draft board clerk for permission to leave the country. The clerk refused. I pleaded with her that teaching in Nigeria was serving my country, and warranted deferring (not replacing) my obligation to the Armed Forces for two years. But my pleas fell on deaf ears; she denied my request. I was deeply disappointed and prepared myself to be drafted into the Armed Forces, which the clerk said would happen shortly.

A few weeks later, I was ordered to report for the "Armed Forces Physical Examination" on September 6. I didn't understand why the Armed Forces needed me at that time. Many young men from Northern Maine were being recruited and drafted, and Aroostook County in particular was certainly more than meeting its quota for soldiers – if there was such a quota.

I became convinced that the clerk had it in for me. It was not unusual for sons of farmers, professional people, and successful merchants to avoid military service altogether. I felt I was not being treated fairly because of my parents' working-class status. This feeling exacerbated my tendency to resent the rich and powerful who use their privileged position to benefit themselves at the expense of poor, old, and sick people.

Good news. On September 2, I received a telegram from Peace Corps Director Sargent Shriver, who wrote that I had "successfully completed initial requirements for service in the Peace Corps." He asked if I could report for training at the University of Michigan October 7, to be part of the first group of volunteers for Thailand. I was ecstatic. I knew little about Thailand – had to look it up on the map – but I was ready to go.

I called the clerk immediately and told her of my Peace Corps invitation. She didn't sound happy, but she would not deny me permission to leave the country for Peace Corps Service. It was one of President Kennedy's high priorities. She instructed me to write her a letter requesting permission to leave the country for Peace Corps Service.

Meanwhile, to my deep consternation, the wheels of the military were turning fast, faster than usual it seemed to me. I had to report for my physical and psychological examinations on September 6, even though I had already requested a deferment, and on September 18, I was notified of my acceptability for the Armed Forces. Soon after, I received my "Order to Report for Induction" in the Armed Forces on October 10. Fortunately, the wheels of the young Peace Corps were moving even faster under Sargent Shriver's sure hand, and I reported for training at the University of Michigan on October 7, three days before I was to be inducted into the Armed Forces.

The Peace Corps secured permission for me to leave the country which the clerk granted a few months before my departure for Thailand. The clerk made it very clear in a little note attached to the permit that it was for one year only, and it would have to be renewed each year. She was not done with me.

Part IV
Peace Corps Training University of Michigan Fall 1961

LEAVING LILLE FOR ANN ARBOR

My world was about to shrink and expand: I would travel halfway around the world in just hours, and I would be stretched by another culture, another language, another way of life. But first I had to get to the University of Michigan in Ann Arbor for three months of training prior to departure for Thailand.

On October 5, 1961, I boarded a small DC-3 World War II relic of a plane in Presque Isle, Maine, about fifty miles from my home. The plane stood on the tarmac with its nose up in the air, its tail close to the ground, eager to take off. The plane's incline was so steep that to get to my seat from the tail section, I had to pull my way up the aisle by grabbing the backs of seats. I felt no anxiety, not about my first plane ride, not about training, and not about whatever lay ahead. I was eager to take off.

The plane's doors closed, the two engines kicked in, and after a brief orientation to the perils of flying, the plane taxied to the end of the runway. With its two engines revved up, the plane roared and shook down the runway, gradually releasing its hold on the land, grabbing at the sky. The plane flew low under the clouds, and I saw rushing below large potato fields like I had worked in, houses like my father and I had built, and green forests like I had explored with my friends. My thoughts drifted from what was ahead to what was behind: my home, my family, and my girlfriend.

I had left home before, but only for college, knowing I would return for Christmas and summer. Other members of my family had left home to work in Connecticut or Massachusetts or elsewhere. My brother Paul had served in the Armed Forces in Germany. But this leaving was different. Peace Corps was new; volunteers would live in small isolated villages and in poor sections of cities; Thailand and Southeast Asia were in the news due to the infiltration of communism in Laos and Northeast Thailand; and our growing, but still small involvement in South Vietnam was worrisome. I knew my parents were concerned, but they had not verbalized it to me – they had not wanted to worry me.

Father R., my pastor, who was on his way to his Bishop in Portland, Maine, had given me a ride to the airport in his fancy black Buick, and had blessed me off. (We had one car which my father had driven to work that morning. If he did not work a day he did not get paid.) Leaving home had not been easy because my mother and father, who seldom displayed emotions, had shown some that morning: My mother had cried as she waved goodbye from the porch, and my father had shed a few tears at his workplace in Van Buren.

What made my departure more painful was leaving my girlfriend, Rolande. We had met in July, and had developed a deep fondness for each other during a two-month courtship. A part of me had wanted to stay with Rolande, but my commitment to service and my desire for adventure had been stronger. We had promised to continue our relationship through letters – the only practical means of communication over long distances in 1961.

My thoughts drifted back to the plane which had slowed to land in Portland, where I was to embark a larger plane for Ann Arbor. I wondered about the training program and the other volunteers. I imagined myself in a small village in Thailand, living with a Thai family, teaching carpentry, speaking Thai, and experiencing the people and their culture. I knew little about what lay ahead.

SURVIVING PEACE CORPS TRAINING

We had been told we were among the very best, selected from tens of thousands who had volunteered. I had received letters from President John F. Kennedy and from U.S. Senator Edmund Muskie (Maine). I had been written up in the St. John Valley Times, the Bangor Daily News and, I think, even in the Boston Globe. The president of the University of Michigan had greeted us enthusiastically, and had set aside a special dorm floor and football tickets for us.

It was easy to forget in the excitement of the farewells, the publicity, and the grand welcome at the University, that I was not yet fully in the Peace Corps. I had volunteered, and I was called a volunteer, but Sargent Shriver's letter was clear: I had been "... chosen to participate in the training program and final selection for a Peace Corps Project in Thailand."

Training was not only about training, it was also about deselection, it was about being sent back home if I didn't measure up. I had been invited and I could be disinvited. Given the large publicity in my small community, returning home and having to explain what happened to my friends at Lawrence's General Store would have been very embarrassing.

Easily forgotten today, as the Peace Corps moves into its sixth decade, is the huge experiment in people-to-people diplomacy that the Peace Corps was in 1961. Many professional diplomats and prominent personages, even the late President Dwight D. Eisenhower, had predicted its failure. In the early days of Peace Corps, being called Kennedy's Kids, was a derogatory term and not the compliment it later became.

Sargent Shriver and his staff believed in us, but they were hardheaded realists. They were going to do everything possible to make sure every unqualified volunteer/trainee was identified and not sent to Thailand. They were equally committed to provide each volunteer with the best training possible. Shriver wanted us to have all the skills and knowledge needed to do an outstanding job. The future of the Peace Corps was very much in our hands. We were going to be scrutinized by the people of Thailand, by officials of the U.S. State Department, and by other groups. The good publicity could quickly turn bad.

Training was tough, highly structured and very full, with little time left for reflection and relaxation at the Tinker Bell bar, although we made it there often enough. There was a high premium placed on acquiring Thai language skills and on evaluating the volunteers. All staff members – I think even the cleaning people – were involved in evaluating us. We had to rank each other in a kind of peer evaluation, a controversial issue among many volunteers. Directing these evaluations was a passel of psychologists and psychiatrists who interviewed us too often and observed us too much.

My highest priorities were to learn Thai language, culture, and history: I spent much time practicing Thai,

Blanche (Corbin) Parent,
Roger's Mom

Blanche (Corbin) Parent, second from right,
May 3, 1924. St. Agathe Daughters HighSchool
from which she received her diploma

Noel Parent,
Roger's Dad

Notre Dame du Mont Carmel Church, Lille, Maine, circa 1910

Roger in winter
clothes, 8 years old

Daughter of Wisdom Sister, teacher, Notre Dame du Mont Carmel
school, Lille, Maine, early 1950's

Noel Parent and cousin
Edmund Parent. Noel's first
car, circa 1930

Notre Dame du Mont Carmel Church, Lille, Maine, Fr. Gelinas, Right, Roger, Altar boy

Lawrence Parent General Store where Roger worked. Lawrence in front, circa 1959

Roger, 7th grade, 12 yrs. Old

Roger's home in winter, Lille, Maine, circa 1956)

Fr. St. Onge, Principal, Van Buren
Boys High School, circa, 1957

Rolande (Ouellette) Parent.
fiancé picture, 1963

Alford Parent, Roger's uncle fiddling in Border
View Manor, Van Buren, Maine, 1990's

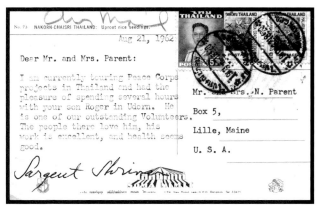

No. 73   NAKORN-CHAISRI THAILAND: Uproot rice seedlings.

Aug 21, 1962

Dear Mr. and Mrs. Parent:

I am currently touring Peace Corps
projects in Thailand and had the
pleasure of spending several hours
with your son Roger in Udorn. He
is one of our outstanding Volunteers.
The people there love him, his
work is excellent, and health seems
good.

Sargent Shriver

Mr. and Mrs. N. Parent

Box 5,

Lille, Maine

U. S. A.

Sargent Shriver post card to Roger's Mom & Dad, July 1962

Roger lived with two families in this house

Women & Children, Village

Thai Style Catholic Church, Bangkok

Roger, second from right on outing with students

Woman working in field

US Marine Tank in Udorn, circa 1962.

Roger (3rd from left) celebrating with villagers

Students studying to be teachers

Roger's students, Udorn Technical school, 1962

Sargent Shriver, Peace Corps Director, center. To his right, U.S.
Ambassador to Thailand, to his left, student. Udorn Technical school.

Teachers College Student

learning how to say Sawaddi Khrab (Hello, Good Morning, etc.) and Kobkhun (Thank you), in and out of the classroom, with tapes and language instructors; I learned many "don'ts" of Thai culture: "Don't cross your legs, don't point your feet at anyone, don't touch the head and shoulder area of a Thai." I thought learning to speak Thai would be easy for me since I had learned English as a second language, but it was not easier for me than for the others.

Training was designed not only to impart skills and attitudes, but also to test the volunteers' psychological mettle. Situations were orchestrated to answer a variety of questions: Was I adaptable? Was I emotionally mature? What were my motivations for joining the Peace Corps? How did I handle stress?

The training staff tried to measure our reactions to the stress they created through a hyper-busy and tightly structured program that left little time to relax, reflect, and recreate. In contrast, our biggest challenge in Thailand was not highly structured busy-ness, but loosely structured work, a relaxed work ethic, and an easy-going social atmosphere. The staff might have gotten a better reading on our ability to handle the stress we were to experience in Thailand by telling us, "Here are the facilities, the teachers, the psychologists, the cultural studies; use these to create your own training program."

Some volunteers didn't do well in training. A few tried too hard to please – they seemed to invent a new persona to impress the training staff. This didn't go over well. As, someone said, "To try to appear smarter than you are is futile because you can never be smarter than you are."

My approach to training was no different than my approach to working at Lawrence's General Store or to working with my father or to tackling university studies. I worked hard, didn't complain, and I strove to treat everyone honestly, courteously, and respectfully. This was not something I had reasoned out as the best approach. This was the way I was raised.

WHAT'S A PEACE CORPS VOLUNTEER?

I didn't know what I was getting into when I volunteered for the Peace Corps, but I wasn't alone – neither did the other volunteers. In October 1961, Peace Corps was only eight months old, and few people knew what the Peace Corps was or was going to be. What was known was that thousands of volunteers were offering their skills, their time, and their enthusiasm for a few years to help people in poor countries. The staff didn't know much more about this new organization than we did; we were the first group of volunteers being trained for Thailand.

The idea of the Peace Corps was not new. William James had discussed it at the end of the 19th century, and it had gained increased viability in the 1950s. Former U.S. Vice President Hubert Humphrey had talked about it in his political campaigns. The Ugly American, by William J. Lederer and Eugene Burdick, had been very popular, and Americans were dismayed over the image of the "loud and arrogant American" overseas who didn't know the local language and flaunted his wealth. (The ugly American in the book is actually a good American.) Many people thought we could find and train individuals who would represent the U.S. better than professional diplomats.

More influential for me than The Ugly American were Dr. Tom Dooley's stories about setting up makeshift hospitals in the jungles of Laos and Vietnam in the 1950s and taking critical services directly to the people. His books, Deliver Us from Evil, The Edge of Tomorrow, and The Night They Burned the Mountain inspired me.

We were engaged in a dangerous Cold War with the Soviet Union, and we wanted and needed to win the hearts and minds of peoples in the less developed world, who the Soviets were actively courting. We wanted to be liked and appreciated for our crucial role in winning the Second World War, and for our generous foreign aid to Europe.

My reasons for joining the Peace Corps were not complicated by Americans' desire to be liked or by the Cold War between us and the Soviet Union. I wanted to improve America's image abroad, and I wanted to lessen tensions in the world. Perhaps I also wanted to leave Lille and have an exotic adventure. Maybe I wanted to test my stamina, resilience, and adaptability. But I wasn't thinking about that. My goal, as I knew it, was to help poor people in a developing country by sharing my skills for a few years.

No one knew for sure the qualities, the personality or the makeup of the ideal volunteer. There were only a few hundred volunteers in the field, and they had been in their assignments only weeks or months; there was little experience to draw on. My idea of a successful Peace Corps volunteer was probably as legitimate as that of the program director and the trainers – maybe even more so. I thought a successful Peace Corps volunteer would be one who lived modestly, provided needed skills, knew the local language, was respectful of the culture, and did not try to impose "our way of life" on the people. With the help of the training staff, I would take my skills, my attitudes, my ideals and my ambitions and shape those qualities into an effective volunteer.

In Thailand, I would help determine the reality and public image of Peace Corps for years to come.

THE FBI AGENT COULDN'T
SPEAK FRENCH

Peace Corps had a problem. They didn't know much about me, nor did they know much about the other volunteers invited to the training program for Thailand. What they knew about me was what I had told them in a long paper questionnaire, and what a few people I had asked for references had written about me. The Peace Corps had to quickly find out if they had by chance recruited a kook or an unsavory character or an unstable personality.

To expedite the investigation of volunteers, the Peace Corps had engaged the FBI to do the background checks while we were in training. The FBI was used only for months – less than a year I think – until a private agency was hired; the Peace Corps was most reluctant to be connected with the FBI in any way.

While I was training at the University of Michigan, an FBI agent (I'll call him Roscoe) arrived in Lille, poked around, and stopped at a neighbor of mine. Roscoe knocked on Mina's door, asked if she knew me and if so, would she mind answering a few questions. Mina didn't speak or understand English (her only language was

French) and all she could make out was my name.

Roscoe didn't know it, but he was in a "foreign land." Not only would he need someone to translate, he would need to interpret the answers carefully, for he was a stranger – an outsider – in Lille. He would not get anyone to make unfavorable comments about me or anyone else in the community. Until the 1970s, French was unofficially the official language in Lille and in other communities of the St. John Valley. (The Valley is bisected by the St. John River, with one side in New Brunswick and one side in Maine.) In Lille, business and social activities were conducted in French.

After attempting without success to communicate with Roscoe, Mina did what she always did when she needed help to read or write letters – she walked the agent across U.S. Route 1 to my mother. Mina woke my mother from her afternoon nap, and told her the man was asking about me, and she couldn't understand a word he was saying.

Roscoe introduced himself and told my mother he was in Lille to ask questions about my fitness to be a Peace Corps Volunteer. When my mother told Roscoe I was her son, he was surprised, and likely wondered whether he should ask her to translate the interview with Mina, knowing the resulting information could be seen as tainted. Maybe he entertained the idea of finding someone else to interview or to translate, but if he did, he did not follow through. He interviewed Mina with my mother as translator. The Peace Corps and the FBI were under intense pressure to complete the background checks quickly; the training program was in progress, and any decision to accept or reject me could not be delayed very long.

Roscoe need not have worried that the interview would be tainted or biased; my scrupulously honest mother would have given him the full truth about me – warts and all – no matter the stakes for me. But Roscoe was not interviewing my mother, he was interviewing her friend Mina, and there's no way Mina would have said anything negative about me, especially to an FBI agent who couldn't speak French.

TEACHING A MAINE ACADIAN FRENCH TO SWIM

I couldn't swim, I couldn't float, I had no way of saving myself or anyone else in water. I had to learn to swim before the end of training. That's what the Peace Corps said.

The Peace Corps assumed that most volunteers during their assignment would likely be near water, on water, and in water; swimming would be a vital survival skill. They didn't know I would be assigned to the driest area in Thailand's Northeast, and would rarely be near water . . . except when I was in a small craft crossing the Mekong River to Laos after the U.S. State Department had ordered all Americans out of that country – but that's another story.

The instructors kidded: "How can a person from Maine, with thousands of lakes, streams, rivers, and hundreds of miles of coastline (3,378 miles when stretched out) not know how to swim?" They didn't know I lived 150 miles from the coast and had never seen it. They didn't know that the waters in Northern Maine's lakes and rivers are ice cold most of the summer, and that I didn't like to put my body in cold water. They didn't know there were no swimming pools and no swim instructors in the far north of Maine. They didn't know that no one in my family knew how to swim.

I was the swim instructor's greatest challenge; whenever I let myself go limp in the water, I sank like a brick. If the instructor, holding me prone to help, let go, I sank. This might be bad physics, but I thought it had something to do with the nature of my body and of water – something I couldn't help. I almost got an inferiority complex about learning to swim.

I wasn't afraid of water and I was always willing to try anything the instructors suggested. But in water, I was like a fish out of water. I couldn't coordinate my leg movements with my arm strokes, I breathed in when my mouth was in water and breathed out when my mouth was out of water. On land, I was well-coordinated, had excellent reflexes, and performed well, but in water I was totally discombobulated.

My exasperated instructor finally gave up trying to teach me how to swim; he decided to teach me a simple water survival technique. He suggested the following: hang loose in the water, bend down, grab your feet, and keep your head under water; you will feel yourself floating with your back exposed to the surface; come up for air and repeat the process. I tried this and to my great surprise it worked: I floated. He said that in an emergency, I should use this approach until someone came to save me; I could survive indefinitely in temperate water, or until a shark got me.

Having learned this survival technique, I started moving around underwater and discovered I could propel myself forward. So in a way, I learned to swim, but only under water, and only as long as my lungs held out. For many years on the Fourth of July at a friend's house, I raced my friend Jackie: I swam under water and she swam above. Sometimes I won.

Peace Corps training was very good, but couldn't teach a French Acadian from Northern Maine to swim.

BEING SHY IS OKAY

I had been told too often when growing up that I was shy. Relatives said, "Oh, you're so shy and cute," and occasionally they talked about my shyness as if I was not present: "He'll get over his shyness as he grows up." Did they think calling me shy would make me less shy? Did they think because I was quiet and reticent that I was oblivious to what was going on around me? Calling me shy just made me more self-conscious. If the people around me had ignored my shyness, I might have grown out of it as a child instead of having to grapple with it as an adult, when it had become more ingrained in my personality – when I saw myself as a shy person and acted accordingly.

A wonderful thing happened to me during Peace Corps training: I discovered that being shy was okay. The Thais liked my reticence, reserve, cautiousness, and sensitivity. I was the antithesis of the popular caricature of the American abroad: loud, backslapping, and insensitive to people of other nationalities and cultures. The Thai staff said I would get along great in Thailand for I acted like a Thai, and I would fit in very well.

I learned that shyness in one culture doesn't necessarily translate to shyness in another; a typical American

can seem too aggressive in Thailand, while a shy American can be seen as a typical Thai. I felt fully accepted by the Thai staff – shyness and all – and this made me more confident. Finally, I was in a situation where my shyness was a strength, not a weakness. Being shy helped me to navigate the training program. My sensitivity to other people's feelings, which had often hindered me in social relations, helped me to avoid cultural faux pas. My wait-and-see attitude before jumping into unfamiliar social situations was a plus. These helped me "cross over" to the Thai culture.

The Thais taught me that my shyness was just fine, and from them I learned to accept myself more fully, and to not let my shyness get in the way of doing what I wanted to do with my life.

I'M ON THE BUS—
ANN ARBOR TO BANGKOK

I had survived the training program and the selection process; I was a full-fledged and bona fide Peace Corps Volunteer. I had sent home my winter clothes, kept only what I needed for the bus trip to the airport, and what I would need for my return from Thailand to Maine or to wherever I would be going after two years of service. But I wasn't thinking about that, I was thinking about my good fortune to be on the bus, and I was sad for the ten volunteers who didn't make it.

Much in life is due to chance and chance had much to do with my being a Peace Corps Volunteer. It was not by design that I was born into a bilingual family and village, that my father taught me carpentry skills, that I learned easily, and that my parents preferred for me a college in Canada. These factors were important, perhaps decisive, in the pre-selection process that got me invited to Peace Corps training. Nor did I have much to do with my natural inclination to work hard or with my high energy level; these characteristics were likely stamped in my genes.

My home didn't only foster in me a shy and reticent personality, it also bred in me a resolute self-confidence; it did so by stressing academic success, by teaching excellent manual skills, and by promoting good health. Working at Lawrence's General Store, where I learned to deal with many kinds of people, was also a confidence builder. Most important were my parents. They loved me and I knew it. They trusted me and my brothers and sisters to make important decisions, and I knew it.

I'm guessing about my makeup. The attitudes and energy, the strengths and weaknesses that make me who I am are not readily traceable to one or two or three factors. Nurture was important and helped shape the dispositions I inherited from my parents, my grandparents, and my other ancestors. Who knows – maybe the experiences of a prior life also helped to shape me. I don't know if I believe in reincarnation, as many Buddhists do, but my two years in Thailand made me appreciate their beliefs and way of life.

I was awakened from my pleasant daydreaming upon arriving at the airport. I got off the bus and into the plane with passport and visa in hand, ready for the long trip to Bangkok. We were greeted as celebrities by the crew and stewardesses (flight attendants today) because we were among the first Peace Corps Volunteers, and because the Peace Corps was constantly in the news. We were going to Thailand to live a simple life, maybe even a spartan life, but we were going there in style.

We flew from Detroit to San Francisco, dined at Fisherman's Wharf, stayed overnight, and embarked another plane for Wake Island, where we would refuel. As we approached Wake Island, I saw broken, rusting, half-sunken ships offshore – relics of World War II – which reminded me of my uncles and other young men from Lille who had fought, who were maimed, and who had died in the South Pacific. Now I was retracing their steps, but on a different and more hopeful mission–a mission to work for peace in a different way.

Once the plane had taxied to a stop at the end of the runway, we ran to the ocean, a few hundred feet away, and soaked our feet in the warm waters of the Pacific. The air was hot and humid, very unlike the cold and dry air of my Northern Maine home. Right off, I loved the hot and humid weather.

HONG KONG

From Wake Island we flew to Hong Kong by way of a quick refueling stop in Tokyo, where we were packed into a small room and not allowed to walk around the airport for respite from the long plane ride. I didn't understand why we needed a visa to walk around the airport – I was naive about such matters. After a few hours in that cramped room we boarded the plane for Hong Kong, where we were to sleep prior to arriving in Bangkok. We could have flown directly to Bangkok, but the welcoming ceremonies at the Don Muang Airport had been scheduled for next day, and we had to arrive exactly on time.

I didn't rest in Hong Kong. I wasn't about to waste sixteen hours in a hotel room in one of the more exotic cities in the world. I left my bags in the hotel and started walking around Kowloon with a few other volunteers. We tried the rickshaw – a light two-wheel vehicle pulled by a person. But I was ill at ease using a human being as a beast of burden to haul me around, and I let him go with a fat tip after a short ride. So did the other volunteers.

We took the Star Ferry across Repulse Bay to Hong Kong Island, and started walking up the nearest tall hill for a bird's-eye view of Hong Kong, Kowloon, and the

Harbor. I think the name of the hill is Victoria. At the base of the hill, we stopped to eat my first real Chinese food. I had eaten Canadianized Chinese dishes in Antigonish, Nova Scotia, where I had attended college, and my mother had made a chop suey concoction, but these had no relationship to genuine Chinese food, to which I took an immediate liking.

As we continued our trek up Victoria Hill night descended, creating a moving panorama of blinking lights from Chinese junks in the harbor, moving lights from cars on the streets below, and electric lights from buildings on hillsides, all faintly outlined by a half moon and zillions of bright stars. Midnight came and went and we kept walking up; I was entranced by the scenery, by the quiet of the night, and by the beauty of the sky. Finally, around 4:00 a.m., we reached the top of the hill, weary and in wonder of our presence on top of Victoria Hill in Hong Kong.

We descended slowly to the head of the Peak Tramway, a railway car hauled up the hill with steel cables powered by electric motors. As we waited for the first morning run around 5:00 a.m., I rested on a bench and watched the bright red rising sun chase away the darkness of night and its bright lights. Now I was ready to return to the hotel, the bus, and the airport for Bangkok.

There was no time to lose; the bus would leave the hotel in about four hours. The downhill ride on the tramway, a run to the ferry, the trip across the bay, and a cab ride to the hotel took a little less than two hours. I quickly shopped for light-weight pants and shirts, ran to the hotel, got into some fresh clothes, grabbed my bags, and got on the bus.

Hong Kong introduced me to Southeast Asia: New geography, new culture, new people, authentic Chinese food, and human beasts of burden. Maybe this rest stop was more important than I had first thought; maybe it was for more than convenience; maybe it was intended to give me a taste of the changes to come in Bangkok and Udorn.

Part V
Peace Corps Volunteer 1961 To 1963

BANGKOK

January 22, 1962 – my 23rd birthday – and I was just minutes from Bangkok. I couldn't have wished for a better gift.

As the plane made its final approach, the excitement among the 45 volunteers was palpable. We had trained in Ann Arbor for three months which had seemed too long, and we were scheduled for two weeks of orientation in Bangkok which seemed unnecessary. My excitement was tempered by my impatience to be teaching in Udorn, but my impatience was easily trumped by the reality and joy of arriving in Thailand.

It had been only a year and two days since President John F. Kennedy's inauguration and challenge to the American people, " . . . ask not what your country can do for you; ask what you can do for your country." I had seized his challenge, made it mine, and had written President Kennedy of my interest in the Peace Corps, then only an idea. By March 1, 1961, when the Peace Corps was created, tens of thousands of Americans had sent letters like mine to the President and Peace Corps Director, Sargent Shriver.

The long flight from Ann Arbor to Bangkok had

been comfortable and uneventful. The pilot had dipped the plane slightly when crossing the international dateline west of Wake Island, awakening the butterflies in my belly, and he had said jokingly, "We've just lost a day." I would have to wait a few years to get back my lost day, but meanwhile, I would learn lessons and create memories that would help shape the rest of my life.

We had flown westward to exotic Southeast Asia, and after a soft landing, we were on the tarmac, taxiing quickly to the terminal. We gave the crew a loud ovation for a great ride over the ocean but, inside, we were celebrating our arrival in Thailand.

The stairway was rolled to the plane, the door was opened, and the regular passengers disembarked. We lined up from the door to the bottom of the stairway for the welcoming remarks and picture-taking. My immediate sensation on walking out was of the heat and humidity. It felt good. As my eyes adjusted to the blinding sunlight, I saw a crowd of Thai officials, American Embassy personnel, and reporters gathered to greet us. We had arrived.

I don't remember what came first, but we sang the Thai National anthem in Thai, and Thai officials welcomed us in English. Volunteers Art and Peggy responded to the welcome in Thai, expressing our happiness at being in Thailand and our gratitude to the Thai people for their invitation to live among them. I was told later that our arrival had doubled the number of Thai-speaking Americans in Thailand. Not only could we sing the Thai national anthem, but we could speak Thai well enough to carry on a rudimentary conversation. The Thais and the American Embassy personnel were impressed with our language skills, but they were even more impressed that most of us were to be assigned upcountry, outside Bangkok.

It would be hard to overestimate the impact of 45Americans singing the Thai national anthem in Thai on the assemblage at the airport, and on Thai peoples across the country in January, 1962. News of the Thai-speaking Americans spread quickly throughout Thailand as the welcoming activities stretched out for two weeks. Our ability to speak Thai, our knowledge of the culture – even if quite elementary – personified the Peace Corps approach. It said that Peace Corps Volunteers respected the culture, the language, the religion, and the way of life of the Thai people. Later, our simple lifestyle would deepen these initial impressions.

FRIED BANANAS

I can still taste those delicious fried bananas. After lunch or dinner during the Bangkok orientation, I had fried bananas for desserts and snacks. I bought them from betel-nut-chewing, blackened-teeth old women squatting on the street. Stubby bananas were peeled, sliced sideways in half, rolled or dipped in batter, and fried in a wok full of oil brought to a boil over hot charcoals. They were crisp and greasy on the outside, mushy and sweet on the inside. They were my energy food.

Eating fried bananas was only half the fun: the other half was watching the women prepare the bananas, and learning to negotiate a fair price in my basic Thai. Most Americans don't like to bargain over prices, and I didn't either when I arrived in Thailand. I soon learned though, that buying and selling meant more than money for the seller and goods for the buyer; it meant conversation, connection, and relationship. If I forgot to bargain a lower price for my fried bananas, I saw disappointment in the eyes of the old betel-nut-chewing-woman – a disappointment I couldn't exactly identify. Did she think I felt superior to her since I didn't take time to connect? Did she think me a sucker for paying a higher price than necessary? Or was it simply a letdown in being deprived the enjoyment of negotiating a price?

I ate fried bananas often, and I grew to enjoy all Thai foods, especially rice, which continues to be part of my favorite meals. Thai meals revolve around rice; an invitation to eat a meal in Thailand, translated literally, means "come and eat rice." Rice was my main food. Three or four different dishes of chicken, fish, pork, eggs, and vegetables were eaten with liberal amounts of rice; many different spices, curries, and sauces were used. I loved the mix of cuisines – Thai, Laotian, Indian, Chinese – but I experienced the great variety of foods in Thailand mainly at festivals or as a guest in homes of better-off people or in expensive restaurants in Udorn.

The meals of many poor families, especially those in the villages of the Northeast, consisted mainly of sticky (glutinous) rice and spicy fish sauce, and possibly a few eggs or pieces of chicken or pork. Sometimes a meal was only sticky rice and spicy fish sauce. Generally, the meals I ate in the school cafeteria, at home, and on the street were simple fare. Even the variety of seasonal fruits available in the Northeast was limited, except for bananas, which were available year-round.

During my first few months in Thailand, I missed the typical meat-and-potatoes American meals – not in a psychological sense, but in the empty-stomach-feeling sense one can have after eating a lot of rice and vegetables, but not much meat. (Most Thai meals in the U.S. include much larger portions of meat and fish than meals in Thailand.) I craved the heaviness of the food back home and the sweet American desserts: pies, doughnuts, and cakes. Fried bananas satisfied my craving for a full stomach and for sweets during my first months in Thailand.

However, it didn't take me long to fully adjust to the Thai foods of the Northeast, and it didn't take me long to realize this was healthy eating at its best. I was rarely sick during my two years in Thailand: no colds, no flu, and few stomach incidents. Today, I eat rice in abundance and eat in Thai restaurants often. Nothing beats a good Thai meal and a bottle of Singha beer, but I miss those fried bananas.

ON THE TRAIN TO UDORN

My memory of the two-week orientation in Bangkok – lectures, parties, celebrities, palaces, chanting monks, and boat rides on the klongs (canals) – is dim and disordered. The eager anticipation of my assignment deflected my attention from parties and tourist activities. I was not a tourist and I didn't want to be one. I wanted to be teaching in Udorn.

Nonetheless, some first impressions of Bangkok are forever impressed on me: the friendly and gracious reception, the women who prepared the fried bananas, the saffron-robed monks who begged food house-to-house each morning, and ants crawling in the rice bowl at a celebrity picnic. (Art, a volunteer, and I looked at the rice, checked out the ants, and without a word took a huge amount of rice . . . the spicy curry would kill the ants.)

At first, the Peace Corps had been hesitant to assign volunteers to the Northeast, Thailand's poorest region, and we were told, its toughest. The Northeast was an area many Bangkok Thais had never visited, and most would not have wanted to live and work there. But Art, Jack, and I were happy to be assigned to Udorn, the most important provincial capitol in the Northeast.

I saw my assignment to Udorn as an expression of confidence in my ability to live and work successfully in a difficult area. There were no paved roads connecting Udorn (population approximately 35,000 in 1961) to any other city or town. Dry goods and foodstuffs typically wanted by Americans, but not necessarily needed, were not readily available. Temperatures ranged from very hot – above 100 degrees to the low 50s – very cold for Thailand; and communists from nearby Laos and China were allegedly gaining influence in the Northeast.

Art and Jack and I were on the train for twelve hours, but we didn't spend much time together; we sat apart from each other to more readily meet Thais and to practice our basic Thai language. I introduced myself to individuals, to families, and to Thai soldiers. I was a falang (foreigner), but my way was different from other falangs: I spoke Thai and I was not loud; I asked questions about family, work, Buddhism, and Thailand. The people seemed to appreciate my desire to learn about them.

Children and their parents asked questions about my family and about America; they taught me new words and phrases, and encouraged me to speak Thai. They complimented me when I got the correct tone on a new word – the tone on a word determines its meaning – and when I mistakenly said knee instead of rice, they laughed. Maybe the going would get tough later, maybe I would experience culture shock, but I was having fun on the train being a Peace Corps Volunteer and I wasn't concerned with the future.

My Carpentry Skills Aren't Needed

My first day teaching in a Thai classroom was my first day teaching in any classroom. I was fresh out of college, not prepared to teach except for three months of Peace Corps training. I didn't know what to expect. I was surprised by the extreme deference given to teachers by Thai students; when a student knelt by my desk to ask me a question, I didn't quite know how to react. I was uncomfortable with this kneeling practice and told my students it was not necessary to kneel. I was intent on learning and abiding by Thai customs, but not this one.

I was supposed to teach carpentry, but my first assignment was to teach English as a second language. There was no need for a teacher of carpentry at the Udorn Trade School. My principal, Pricha, had been told by the Government Ministry that he was getting a Peace Corps Volunteer, and as far as I could tell, he hadn't had much say in the matter. Nevertheless, he was thankful for a volunteer because there was some prestige attendant to having an American teacher in his school.

It should have been evident, even to the faraway planners in the Peace Corps' Washington office and to the

Thai government ministry in Bangkok, that Thai carpentry skills and practices more than met Thailand's current needs. Some of their skills, particularly those needed to work with very hard woods, such as teak, and those needed to use their "ancient" tools, were superior to those of most American-trained carpenters, and certainly to mine. Thai carpenters did not need to know how to install built-in ovens, stove tops or other newfangled devices in the early 1960s.

The principal, my Thai colleagues, and I never talked about this dilemma. We handled this thorny issue through a combination of the Thai way and my way: Non-direction and non-confrontation by them and low-key persistence by me. Some volunteers were frustrated by these ill-defined job situations, which were fairly common in the early days of the Peace Corps, and are still too common today. Volunteers got even more frustrated when they tried to resolve these situations in a typically aggressive American way. Some volunteers, unable to resolve these situations satisfactorily, asked for reassignment and, in later groups, some returned home. All volunteers in the first Thailand group completed their tour. When I was a Peace Corps Volunteer, nothing would have led me to ask for a change of assignment or to return home early, except a catastrophic illness.

When I sensed that my principal did not quite know what to do with me, I suggested visiting each classroom and workshop and introducing myself to the students and the teachers to get to know everyone. This solved for a while the mis-assignment and the scheduling dilemma created by my arrival at the Trade School in the middle of the school year.

During this self-styled orientation, it quickly came to me that I had other skills which could benefit the school. The teacher/librarian asked me if I would help organize the books. While working in the library, I wrote to publishers in the United States for materials on carpentry, construction, plumbing, electrical wiring, auto-mechanics and so on. Many of the companies sent books, and the library grew considerably.

I taught English as a second language (ESL) not only at the Trade School, but also at the Girls' Handicraft School. I hadn't been trained to teach ESL, but my Peace Corps colleague, Art, who had been trained in this field, assisted me. Also, I felt confident of my ability to teach English since I had learned English as a second language. My good friend Art joked that my students spoke English with a French Acadian accent; it was probably true. I've not completely lost my French accent, because I learned to speak English from French nuns who spoke English with a French accent.

The carpentry teacher asked if I would assist him to teach certain aspects of carpentry, i.e., how to figure out the pitch and dimensions of a roof. I became a resource person for this teacher, fulfilling somewhat my original assignment to teach carpentry. I amassed a very full schedule of teaching and activities, and soon the daily trips on my Peace Corps-issued bicycle took too much time. I was pedaling some 15 to 25 miles each day, going from one school to the other, and to other activities. I bought a small motor scooter with funds saved from my living allowance, which allowed me to get much more done. I continued to use my bicycle to go here and there.

Today, it almost takes an act of God for Peace Corps to allow a volunteer to use a motor scooter or motorbike – too many volunteers have been killed or maimed in motorbike accidents. When I was a volunteer, there were few rules because we were making up the Peace Corps as we were going along. Today, too many rules have drained some of the imagination and fun out of the

Peace Corps. Decades later, when I directed Peace Corps programs in Haiti, Grenada, and Bulgaria, I saw that the Peace Corps had become a hidebound bureaucracy – maybe necessary – but the Peace Corps could not have been established by the bureaucracy it is today.

CHINA SAYS PEACE CORPS
VOLUNTEERS ARE SPIES

In January 1962, I didn't understand why the People's Republic of China was bothered by the Peace Corps, a small and fledgling government organization of volunteers, often called amateurs by professionals in diplomacy. Today, I understand better why China was bothered, indeed threatened, by the Peace Corps. It is a powerful idea: ordinary Americans volunteering to live simply among the people of poor countries, learning the culture and the language, accepting people as they are, not as they might want them to be, and free to speak as they wish, not obligated to support their country's policies, unlike professional diplomats.

The Peace Corps staff in Bangkok had told us that China was accusing Peace Corps of being an arm of the Central Intelligence Agency (CIA), saying that its volunteers were spies of "paper tiger" America. I didn't take this seriously and laughed at the idea: Me, a spy? But in Udorn, I myself heard Thai language radio broadcasts from China that Peace Corps Volunteers were spies.

I knew about the cold war and the intense competition in armaments and ideas between the Soviet Union and the United States, but I wasn't very sensitive to, nor did I care much about the geopolitical machinations of my government or any other. My concern was about helping the people of Thailand and about my work, not what China said about the Peace Corps. I understood, however, that these accusations could seriously harm the Peace Corps and hinder my acceptance in Udorn. If China and other Communist nations had been able to convince the world that the Peace Corps was a cover for the CIA, it could have ruined it. Most governments would have been very reluctant to accept volunteers if they had thought the Peace Corps was a part of the CIA and most Americans would have stayed away from volunteering for the Peace Corps. I would not have volunteered for an organization with a reputation for spying.

To counter these false accusations, the Peace Corps immediately established policies not to hire ex-CIA officers, and the CIA itself was forbidden from hiring former Peace Corps Volunteers for five years after their service. These policies were effective in rebutting the more egregious accusations of spying, and as far as I know, they're still followed today.

Still, at the dawn of the Peace Corps, more than policies were needed to clearly establish its independence from the CIA, and to convince my Thai colleagues and friends I was not a spy. This was especially difficult in Udorn, where a large number of CIA officers worked and lived. (They were affiliated with Air America, the CIA's "Air Force.") Moreover, it was difficult for Thais to understand why I would leave my seemingly rich American life to work and live in Udorn; the American spirit and tradition of volunteerism was not well known in Thailand.

Thais knew Americans as courageous soldiers from World War II. I wanted to show another side of America. I strived to establish a reputation for myself and the Peace

Corps as one dedicated to peace through service. I maintained a strict separation between myself and agents of the CIA and advisors of the U.S. Army. I refused invitations for American meals and beer at the Army and CIA base near the airport – difficult to refuse and difficult to explain; I hope they didn't think I thought myself too good for them.

Eventually, the radio broadcasts from China ceased. The broadcast's couldn't compete with our day-to-day presence in schools, villages and towns, and with our living among the people we served.

BAKING A CAKE
IN A CHARCOAL OVEN

My girlfriend Rolande wrote letters to me all the time and I responded in kind. We loved each other and still do, even more so. Once, she surprised me with a big box of goodies mailed all the way from Van Buren, Maine – a box full of Hersheys, Snickers, and Almond Joy candy bars; and boxes of cake mix: yellow and chocolate, I think; and a beautiful onyx ring. I've never worn the ring, and can't find it today. I don't like to wear rings and trinkets, but I wear my wedding ring and I hope that has made up for losing the ring she gave me as a sign of her love more than fifty years ago.

The cost of retrieving the parcel from the Udorn Post Office made a big dent in my volunteer stipend and I had to tell her not to send another. She purchased the stuff, paid to mail it, and I had to pay to retrieve it. Peace Corps Volunteers did not have diplomatic privileges, so when the parcel arrived, I had to pay a stiff tariff. But when I opened the package and saw the candy bars and the cake mix and the love ring and the love letter, I quickly forgot the cost.

My colleagues Art and Jack and I ate some chocolate bars, savoring the missed taste, and stored the balance away in a place where ants couldn't get them. If we left food unprotected anywhere, ants would get to it in minutes. Fighting ants was something I learned on the job – there were few ants in my Northern Maine home, and ants had not been covered in Peace Corps training. Our neighbor told us to keep ants away from the table by placing small vessels of water under its legs. When the ants learned to walk across the water on the backs of dead ants, cleaning the "moat" became an added chore.

We didn't know what to make of the cake mix because we had no oven. When we cooked our meals we did so on traditional clay pot stoves using charcoal for fuel, but we didn't cook often – we didn't have to. During the first weeks after our arrival our dinners were brought to us from the Teacher Training College cafeteria, our lunches were provided in our schools, and we ate out occasionally.

Soon after I received my package of goodies, two freelance reporters dropped in to talk about our Peace Corps work for a magazine. Since they didn't have a place to stay, we offered them room to sleep and dinner, and gave each a precious candy bar. In the morning, while we were out teaching, they ate all the remaining candy bars, left the wrappers on the floor, and took off without even writing a thank-you note. We never heard from them again nor did we hear of an article they were to write. I guess they were moochers, not reporters.

Now that we had no more candy bars to satisfy our sweet tooth, we turned our attention to the cake mixes. A colleague of Art's had told him that small ovens using charcoal for fuel were available in the market, so He set out to buy one. Sure enough, he found an oven, bought it and brought it home with visions of cake in our heads. The oven was made of tin, about 18 inches deep, 12 inches wide, and 12 inches high; it had double walls, bottoms, and tops – sort of a box within a box – with a tray at the bottom for the hot charcoal. This far-less-than-airtight contraption allowed hot air to circulate from the charcoal tray up and around the inner tin box to cook what was inside.

We had not thought about a tin to bake the cake, so I went to the store for one, and for eggs and powdered milk needed for the mix. This was growing into a big project which generated much interest from our neighbors, who always seemed to know everything going on in our house. I stirred the ingredients in a bowl while Art started the coals in our clay pot stove and transferred them to the oven tray. With exact timing rarely seen since, my batter was ready when Art's fire was ready, and I poured it in the tin and placed it in the oven.

Now we thought all we had to do to eat our treat was to wait, but we were just starting our cake-baking. The oven lost so much heat through cracks at its joints and through its thin walls that Art had to stoke the charcoal in the tray and replenish the coals constantly. There was no window in the oven door, so checking the progress of the cake meant opening the door often and losing much heat. This prolonged the cooking time far beyond the recipe's estimated 35 minutes.

After the cake had been in the oven 25 minutes or so, the batter was still bubbly. We piled more red-hot lumps of charcoal in the tray, and after another 15 minutes, a thin skin had formed on top, and after 15 more minutes a tan crust had appeared – we were making progress. We decided to not open the oven door for a while and to stoke the fire to a higher temperature. A half hour later we opened the door to a beautiful dark brown cake; it hadn't risen much, but it looked very tasty.

I pulled the cake out of the oven, placed it on the table and let it cool. Since the cake had separated from the walls of the tin, I turned it over, and out came the cake with what seemed like a little bounce as it hit the table. Neither one of us had ever baked a cake before, and as far as we knew, every cake had a bounce when dropped from a pan. I took a regular table-knife to cut a piece, but I couldn't get the rounded end of the knife into the cake. Art handed me a sharp pointed knife which I forcefully inserted in the cake to cut a few pieces.

I opened my mouth and clamped my jaws in a piece, but could hardly bite off a chew; our cake was so hard and rubbery that neither Art nor I could masticate a bite into something swallowable or digestible. I don't know what we had done wrong: Maybe it was the oil we had forgotten or maybe it was the extra-long cooking time or maybe it was the atmospheric pressure or maybe we were inept cooks or maybe it was all of the above. Whatever. We couldn't eat the cake, so we played catch with it and bounced it off the wall until it disintegrated into small pieces that stray dogs ate, They seemed to like it.

It didn't matter. We soon stopped missing cake and candy bars, and hungered for fried rice and sticky rice and chicken curry and thousand-year-old eggs and durian ice cream and rice whiskey and sweet ovaltine and Singha beer and fried bananas.

TOO DRUNK TO RIDE MY BIKE

There was no law against riding a bike drunk, there was no .008 or .01 rule, but I had to be able to mount my bike and pedal it, and after having too much to drink that one night, I couldn't. So I asked the owner of my favorite the ice cream shop next door to keep my bike overnight, and I rode home in a samlow – a three-wheel bicycle built for two or three passengers.

My first experience using a taxi powered by a human "beast of burden" had been in Hong Kong, and I had felt so uneasy I had gotten off after scant yards and had given the guy a big tip. After being in Thailand for a while, I had come to realize that hiring a samlow was at times the only practical means of getting around; it was a way for young men (and not so young men) to earn a living.

I had been warned that drinking alcoholic drinks in very hot weather could get one drunk faster than drinking the same amount in a cold clime. I had never been a heavy drinker, and didn't even know my limits in cold Northern Maine. Anyway, what are warnings for if not to be forgotten at the exact time one should not?

A few Thai soldiers had invited me from my ice cream treat to the "Jukebox" next door for a few Singha beers. I had met the soldiers a few days earlier at the Trade School: Kidsad was captain of an artillery battalion, and the other was a mortar officer. I think his name was Naron. Kidsad spoke some English, but we spoke Thai; they enjoyed a conversation in their language with an American.

We spent hours talking about our work and our families while drinking delicious Singha beer. Like me, they had left families behind – theirs in Northern Thailand and mine in Northern Maine. I lost track of time, lost count of the beers, and lost the good sense to know I had drunk too many Singhas. Still, I was aware enough to leave before making a complete fool of myself. On the way out, when I bumped a few chairs and tables, I knew I was in trouble.

The samlow ride took about 20 minutes, long enough for me to start feeling very queasy. I arrived at my home just in time to pay the driver, get out, and puke in the ditch. The full violence of the liquor had taken over, and I felt god-awful terrible. I was even less steady than when I had left the "Jukebox," and could not climb the stairs to the first level of my house, built on stilts about ten feet off the ground. Staying upright was the best thing I could do for my sick stomach, and I leaned against the nearest tree for support.

In my drunken condition, I gradually became aware of an itching and burning sensation spreading from my right shoulder to my arm and back. This sensation grew quickly into pain of such intensity that I yanked myself abruptly from the tree, checked the right side of my body, and saw it covered with red fire ants that had crawled on me for a midnight treat. I tried to brush them off, but hundreds of ants had gotten under my clothes. I bolted up the stairs three steps at a time – the pain had momentarily taken over my drunken stupor – tore off my clothes, jumped in the shower, went to bed, and fell in a deep coma-like long sleep.

Next day was a nightmare to which I wished I hadn't awakened. I had the mother of all hangovers, my stomach was churning, and my right shoulder and arm were swollen and painful. I not only thought I was going to die, I wished to die. I had heard of people with hangovers wishing they were dead, now I understood what they meant. I could not eat ... and did not want to eat for two or three days.

I told my housemates, Art and Jack, what I had done to myself and asked them to get word to my principal that I was too sick to teach. I didn't tell anyone else of my drunken night, but word got around Udorn, and many people had a good laugh. I guess there was no way a Thai-speaking American teacher getting drunk in the "Jukebox," having to leave his bike in the ice cream shop, could get drunk and remain anonymous. I was completely embarrassed and stayed away from the "Jukebox" for months.

BECOMING THE PEACE CORPS
VOLUNTEER I WANTED TO BE

When Art and Jack and I arrived in Udorn, we were provided a comfortable traditional Thai house on the Teacher Training College campus. They were assigned to the Teacher Training College; I was assigned to the Udorn Trade School. The house was made of teakwood, built on stilts about ten feet off the ground. It had three bedrooms, a western-style toilet and shower, a small kitchen, and a living room with one wall of doors which opened to a large veranda that overlooked the campus. It was a great place to relax and speak English after a full day of teaching in a language still foreign to us.

I loved our house, our neighbors, and our camaraderie; I was comfortable. Yet, I was uneasy and dissatisfied with my situation: I was not learning to speak Thai and the local dialect quickly enough, and I was not getting to know my Thai colleagues at the Trade School, where I taught carpentry and English, except on a superficial level. The Trade School occupied a lower social status than the Teacher Training College, and so did its teachers. My residence at the college widened the social gap between my colleagues and me, and made it more difficult to bridge.

I was happy and enjoyed living in Thailand, but I was not living up to my idea of a Peace Corps Volunteer.

I asked Pricha, my principal, if I could have a room in a house owned by the Trade School. He didn't like the idea, saying the house was too old and would not be good enough for me. He thought I would miss living with my Peace Corps friends, have a hard time using the squat toilets, and would dislike "showering" by splashing water on myself from a large jar while wrapped in a pawkama (a sarong type cloth for men, tied at the waist) for privacy. Principal Pricha had studied for some months at the University of Hawaii; he knew the comfortable American lifestyle, and he understood our greater need and desire for personal privacy.

I persisted. I explained to Principal Pricha that living with a Thai family would help me learn the language, the culture, and family life more than was possible living with my two American buddies at the Teacher Training College. This final argument won him over and he relented. He arranged for me to live in a house next door to the school with Charoon and Luk, teachers at the Trade School, and their two young families. Deep down, I think he was very pleased to have his Peace Corps Volunteer living near the school and becoming a more intimate part of his school family.

My new home was a simple and large rambling structure, built with teakwood that had darkened with age inside and outside, giving the house a somber, almost haunting look, particularly at night. It was built on stilts about 5 or 6 feet off the ground – a necessity since the house lay nearly three feet below the grade of the road, a couple hundred feet away. When a big rain fell, water would run off the road, down the lot, under and around our house, forming a pond behind it, where the family would fish. I'm still not sure how fish happened in a pond formed by rain where no pond existed most of the year. According to the people in my house, it just happened.

Windows were simple openings with no glass or screens, but there were wooden shutters hung from the inside, for privacy. Screens were installed in my room to keep the mosquitoes and the bugs out. To Thai people, screens were a western thing, and they didn't want any for themselves. They also provided me with a regular western-style bed and mosquito netting – the mosquitoes made their way to my room despite the screen in the window.

The sitting areas, kitchen, and toilet facilities were common to all. Each family had a large room for sleeping and other private uses, and I had a small bedroom for the same purposes. In addition to my western-style bed, my room had an armoire, a desk with a lamp, and more private space than I had in my Lille home where I grew up with nine brothers and sisters. This large house was covered by a very old and very rusty tin roof which amplified the noise of rain to a thunderous roar.

Adjusting to the squat-type toilets was easy, and bathing in the open by splashing water from a huge jar, while struggling to keep the pawkama from falling off, soon became second nature. There was no western-style shower in the house because of no running water in the house. The water needed to drink, cook, clean house, and wash our bodies came from captured rain or was carried in buckets from sources some distance away. Adjusting to the two families and having little privacy was not a problem for someone raised in a small house with nine siblings.

Living with Charoon's and Luk's families and their children was the best decision I made as a volunteer. I quickly became more proficient in Thai and the local dialect – spoken in our home almost always. I got a first-hand education in Thai family life, how they cared for children and how they related to each other and their extended family members. I also developed closer and deeper relationships with my colleagues at the Trade School.

THANOM'S TANTRUM

Two-year-old Thanom was having a terrible tantrum and no one was doing anything about it. His father and mother were acting as if nothing was happening, as if Thanom was behaving normally. I thought, "They've got to do something about this." He was out of control, screaming and crying and jumping. I imagined he might hurt himself by falling or hitting his head against a wall or he might grow up unable to control his temper. Had he been mine, I would have forced him to settle down – to sit in a corner or something similar. I was 23, and didn't know much.

I was raised a different way. My two-year-old tantrums were not allowed to work themselves out; they were forced to stay under the surface of my personality . . . maybe to come out later in less socially acceptable ways. The Thais thought it best to allow a two-year-old's tantrum to come out when a child was two years old. Thanom's parents seemed to say, "If Thanom has a fit, let him have his fit and get over it." They seemed to understand that the natural behavior of a two-year-old child shouldn't be treated as if the child were an adult – that a two-year old's behavior doesn't necessarily extrapolate to adult life.

It's chancy to speculate whether the child-rearing practices of one culture would work in another. I suppose I was raised to fit into my society, although I've not always felt that I fit in very well. I was not spanked much as a child nor was I unduly restricted in my activities. I was lucky to live in a rural area and to be part of a family of ten children; my parents didn't have time to be excessively concerned with me or any one child.

I'd been living in my new home near the Trade School with two Thai families only a few months when I witnessed Thanom's tantrum. I had been told about the Thais "maj pen raj" attitude to life, but I hadn't seen it in raising children. "Maj pen raj," or in the Lao of the Northeast, "bo pen yang," means: it's ok, it doesn't make any difference, it's all the same, it doesn't matter. This laissez-faire attitude showed itself not only in child-raising, it permeated Thai life.

This easy-goingness derives in part from Buddhism, which advocates a softer and more tolerant approach to life. Its religious and family precepts and rules are mild. At Buddhist ceremonies, I was invited to participate fully. Conversely, my Catholic religion frowned on my participation in Buddhist ceremonies, and prohibited full participation in her ceremonies by Buddhists. Also, the rural character of Thailand in the 1960s provided ample geographical space, which I think translated into psychological space for differences and eccentricities.

The "maj pen rai" attitude made it easier for me to live with Thais, and for them to accept me. If I did something different, like riding my bike at night near cemeteries or if I was too harsh with my students or if I killed cockroaches in my room (they believed in reincarnation and didn't believe in killing), they probably said "maj pen raj – that's his way, it doesn't make any difference."

I enjoyed the "maj pen rai" of the Thais, and the

resulting respect for differences among themselves and those of other cultures. I absorbed much of the easygoing Thai way of life, and when I returned to the United States, I was even more low-key than when I had left two years earlier. Later, I lost some of the easygoing Thai attitude and reabsorbed the more straight-laced and less tolerant American way. Still, I believe that the "maj pen rai" way I absorbed in Thailand made me more sensitive to the different peoples I represented years later when I was a City Councilman and Mayor of South Bend.

LEARNING TO SPEAK THAI

Learning to speak Thai was not as easy for me as I thought it would be. I knew French and English – French I had learned naturally at home and in my community, but English had been forced on me in school. I thought my two vocabularies and knowing the sounds of two languages would give me an edge in learning Thai, but it didn't turn out that way.

Thinking back on it, the way English was forced on me and my fierce resistance to speaking English as a child, may have created an unconscious animosity to learning any other language. I suspect my resistance to learning English stemmed from an innate fear that learning English put at risk my cherished Acadian French way of life in Lille. In the 1940s and 1950s, it would have been realistic to feel this way, for we were treated as second-class citizens by the English-speaking peoples and their dominant culture.

Still, I was as determined to learn Thai as I had been in resisting learning English as a child. Upon my arrival in Udorn, my friend, Charoon, and I made a pact to learn each other's language: I spoke English with him and he spoke Thai with me. When we were not learning quickly enough, we developed another approach. He read a sentence in Thai which I repeated, and I read the translation of that sentence in English which he repeated. We learned correct pronunciation and meanings, and internalized sentence structures rather effortlessly this way. I had to make sure, though, that when Charoon said my pronunciation was correct that it was really so. He had heard mispronounced Thai so often that if I only came close to the correct pronunciation, he would say it was very good. What he meant was that it was good enough.

Thai is not easy to learn: five different tones and different vowel lengths combine to give many possible meanings to the same word. For example, the word "khaw" (spelled phonetically) can have eight different meanings: knee, news, enter, rice, he/she/they and white. I aimed for a perfection in speaking Thai that I didn't reach, but I achieved a very good working knowledge of the language, particularly after I moved into the home of two Thai families.

Learning to speak Thai (or any language) was more than a mechanical translation of an English word into its Thai equivalent. It was taking the world of my Thai friends and colleagues and making it my own; it was entering their work life and their home life; and it was sharing their happy times and their sad times. Learning Thai was also an invitation to my friends and colleagues to learn about me, and to become part of my family and culture.

Knowing Thai was very important, but there's an even more important quality essential to work, to teach, to communicate with people effectively. It's respect for and accepting their culture and way of life; it's having the ability and willingness to put oneself in another person's shoes. Not every Peace Corps Volunteer had that quality. One volunteer had excellent command of the language and knew the culture well, but had a superior air about him – one of condescension and arrogance – that distorted his "vision" and understanding. He did not fully accept the Thais, nor did they fully accept him. He was not very successful in Thailand. Another volunteer was not always tuned to the culture, and never achieved fluency, but she was humble, accepted people as she found them, and had the ability to put herself in other people's shoes – to feel their pain, their pleasures, and their love. She was successful in Thailand.

A U.S. MARINE PROPOSITIONS THAI DOCTOR'S WIFE

No one knew the Marine's name; they knew only that he was tall and white and young and dressed in green fatigues. He had touched Mrs. Sirikhan on the shoulder and he had asked her to go to the Ma Phak Di Hotel nearby. This he had done in broad daylight on Phosi Street at the end of a work day, when it was packed with people shopping and talking with friends as they made their way home.

News of the American Marine's flagrant violation of a cultural and sexual norm had spread quickly, and there was quite a hubbub in the teacher lounge at the Trade School when I arrived. My principal, Pricha, told me the story: a U.S. Marine had propositioned Mrs. Sirikhan, wife of the prominent Dr. Sirikhan, last evening on Phosi Street, and people were outraged. That the Marine had wanted sex was not the issue – frequenting a cathouse in Thailand was a common activity of young men, married men, and old men. For less than a few bucks, the Marine could have had an attractive prostitute. What they couldn't understand was why he had approached and touched a respected woman.

In early 1960s Udorn, most women wore a Thai style sarong, but professional women and the wives of professional men generally wore western-style clothes, and so did the prostitutes who catered to American soldiers. The young Marine didn't know this. The Marines had arrived only a few months earlier, and had not been instructed in Thai culture. A few days before this incident, I had met a Marine in an ice-cream shop who didn't even know he was in Thailand – he knew only he was in Southeast Asia.

Somphon, a teacher, asked half-seriously if it was customary in my country to proposition respectable women on the street for sex. There was joking and awkward laughter, for they knew I was embarrassed by this incident. I was upset and worried that this Marine's gross cultural transgression would reflect on me and my country. Mrs. Sirikhan had never been touched by a man in public, Thai or otherwise. She was shocked, embarrassed, insulted. In Thailand, only a prostitute would allow herself to be touched in public, albeit reluctantly. She was mortified to think the Marine thought her to be a prostitute.

Mrs. Sirikhan spoke English, having lived in the United States a few years when her husband was in medical school. She told the Marine in her soft, no-nonsense voice to leave her alone, and immediately returned home. When her husband learned what had happened he became very upset and angry. He ordered his driver to take him immediately to the Director of the U.S. Information Service (USIS) for the Northeast Region. He demanded apologies from the Marine Commandant and the American Ambassador to Thailand, and requested the Marine's removal from Udorn. The USIS Director had learned by rumor the main facts of the story, and had been trying to contact the Marine Commandant when Dr. Sirikhan arrived. He immediately apologized to Dr. Sirikhan, promised to contact the Marine commandant that very evening, and to transmit Dr. Sirikhan's request to the Ambassador in Bangkok.

The Marine Commandant apologized to Dr. and Mrs. Sirikhan the next day. However, no action was taken to remove the Marine from Udorn and he was never punished. The incident was larger than one Marine, and responsibility went up the Marine hierarchy. If the Marine had been properly oriented to his surroundings, he would not likely have taken Mrs. Sirikhan for a prostitute. The leadership was culpable and would have had to be punished too so, in the end, no one was punished.

Much of my two years in Udorn coincided with the Marines' and CIA's presence, which I learned to ignore. My Thai colleagues and friends and I learned that front-line soldiers are rarely effective diplomats: they can give out candy, build playgrounds and schools, build roads and hospitals, but their training is to defend and protect their country or an ally by maiming and killing the enemy. They're not trained in diplomacy.

I was further convinced that the best way to foster goodwill among nations is to share our education, our skills, our food, and our money to help people create for themselves a decent life.

PRESIDENT JOHN F. KENNEDY SAYS: "DON'T GO TO LAOS."

I hadn't planned to go to Laos, but when I heard I wasn't supposed to go, I wanted to go.

If I'm told to do something, I don't want to do it. If I'm told not to do something, I want to do it. When my kindergarten teacher tried to teach me English I resisted; when my college hall rector turned the lights off at eleven, I bought an extension cord to bring light to my room from the bathroom; and when I decided to run for Mayor of South Bend in 1978, many said I shouldn't run and couldn't win, but I did and I won. So when President Kennedy told Americans to leave Laos in 1962, going to Laos became irresistible.

President Kennedy must have had good reasons to tell American citizens to stay out of Laos. I think it was part of his strategy to keep communism out of Thailand. Months earlier, he had ordered a few thousand Marines to Udorn to send a clear message to the Pathet Lao (Communists) in Laos: "Don't even think of crossing the Mekong River to Thailand." I was aware of the Cold War and the communist threat, but although I had a ringside seat to the worldwide conflict being played out on the small stage of Udorn, I didn't feel the drama at all. I only felt the drama of teaching my students.

When a group of Peace Corps friends came to visit from Khonkaen, we decided to go to Laos for the weekend. My friend, Art, joined us and we took a bus for the 12-mile trip to Nongkai, a small city on the Thailand side of the Mekong River, where we hired a small boat to cross over. It was windy, the river was turbulent, the boat rocked scarily, and I was glad that Peace Corps had taught me how to float.

We had left boldly but arrived timidly. My friends, not expecting to go to Laos, had not brought their passports, and I had not thought to bring mine. To me, crossing the Mekong River to Laos was like crossing the St. John River near my home in Maine to go to Canada; I had not needed a passport to do that. We thought we might be turned back, but there were no border guards to check us. Only a friendly gaggle of vendors selling swaths of brightly colored cloth, trinkets, chicken pieces, and sticky rice were there to greet us.

We boarded a dilapidated bus which hugged the Mekong for a short ride to Vientiane, the capitol city. On the way we encountered a roadblock manned by soldiers wearing red berets, brandishing their old rifles. This made my blood course a little faster, maybe this was the border checkpoint where they would ask for passports, but after peering into the bus, they waved us through without a question. The driver said these were Royal Laotian Army soldiers, loyal to the King of Laos, backed by the American Government. That's why they let us through without interrogation.

Another few miles brought us to another checkpoint – this one manned by soldiers wearing black berets, neutralists in the dispute between the King and the communists. This time the bus driver asked us for money to bribe the soldiers and we gave him a few bahts (Thai currency). He stopped, got out, walked to the captain, said a few words, discreetly handed him our bahts, returned to the bus, and drove off. No questions asked. Money was explanation enough.

There were three seemingly coexisting armies in Vientiane: the King's soldiers in red berets, neutralists in black berets, and communists in camouflaged uniforms. They swaggered in the city, displaying their guns, seeking to keep and to get more power. I remember these soldiers scrutinizing us as we walked about. They knew we were Americans by our dress and demeanor, and probably wondered what we were doing in Laos, but they didn't bother us. When I asked a red-bereted soldier for directions, he smiled and gave me directions. That was it.

Any anxiety I felt melted away quickly as I heard Laotians speak French in shops and restaurants and in a hotel lobby. I immediately felt at home and less a stranger. Laos had been a French colony until the middle 1950s, and I should have realized before I arrived that French would still be an important language in Vientiane. I had learned English in school, but French was my mother tongue – a tongue which still evokes deep feelings of family, home, friends, and community in Northern Maine. It felt good to speak French.

My memories of Vientiane are of friendly people, not oblivious to the three armies in their midst, but wise in knowing that whomever ended up on top would not much affect their day-to-day living at the bottom. In 2002, my wife (Rolande) and I visited our friend, Art, who's married to a Laotian woman, in Vientiane. The daily life of the people had not changed much. They were still one of the poorest populations in the world, and the replica of the French L'Arche de Triomphe still dominated Vientiane. But the communists held the reins of government and American influence made English more important than French. Added to the general misery was the suffering from the unexploded bombs, grenades, and mines which maim and kill hundreds of people each year – a legacy of the Vietnam War. (Thousands of bombs were dropped in Laos to interdict supplies on the Ho Chi Minh trail, and thousands more were dropped by American planes as they were returning from aborted bombing runs over Hanoi, on their way to a safe landing in Udorn.)

The people of Laos seemed no better off than they had been more than forty years ago when I first crossed the Mekong River with no passport. My government's interest in the people of Laos had more to do with the threat of global communism than with helping them. Today, some U.S. assistance trickles in, and some non-government organizations (NGO's) are helping people deal with the killing legacy of unexploded ordnance, but it's a minuscule effort compared to the challenge. The world is small, they say, but the distance between hearts and understanding remains large.

VANG VILLAGE: MEKONG WHISKEY—SICK BABIES—RAW DUCK BLOOD

When Charoon and Luk (my host families) had cautioned me not to use the road by the Buddhist wat (temple) near our home late at night for fear the spirits of those interred there would invade my body and my mind, I had done so anyway. So when I told them I was going to Vang Village alone they were concerned, but did not try to dissuade me. I was eager and ready to travel alone, to get a feel for the people and their ways without the filter of my good hosts' comments and explanations. I wanted to come and go as I pleased.

I had arrived in Thailand nearly four months earlier, in January 1962, spoke Thai fairly well, and I was familiar with the local Lao dialect. My trips outside Udorn had been with Thai friends and colleagues who tended to be overly protective. I understood their concern and appreciated their caring – I was their friend – but I was oblivious to another reason for their protectiveness: not only was I their friend, I was a guest of the Thai government, and one of "Kennedy's Kids," as the first Peace Corps Volunteers were often called. If something had happened to me, it would have been embarrassing to them, to the

Trade School, and to their government.

I was not always sensitive enough to the acute need to avoid embarrassment, to save face, in Thailand. I come from a Northern Maine mix of French-Acadian-Quebec stock where concern for saving face is easily trumped by a strong independent streak. My Thai hosts sensed my need for independence much earlier than I sensed their desire to care for me and to protect me from an incident which could have caused embarrassment.

School was out and nothing much was happening when I took off on my bicycle to visit the small village of Vang, about five or six miles from Udorn. I had traveled to Vang earlier with Charoon and Luk, and the village Headman, Mr. Kasem, had invited me to return. It was a slow and hot day during the hot season.

Temperatures often exceeded 100 degrees Fahrenheit during the hot season – temperatures I had not known in Lille, Maine, or anywhere else. Yet the idea of pedaling and pushing a bicycle for an hour and a half in high heat didn't dampen my enthusiasm. The extreme cold of Northern Maine and the extreme heat of the tropics never bothered me much. I think adapting to extreme temperatures is as much a state of mind as it is a state of biology.

I pedaled to the outskirts of Udorn on paved and graveled streets, continued on dirt roads for about two miles, then turned sharply off the road on a path which meandered across rice paddies, and through partially wooded areas, giving me an occasional shady moment. Keeping myself and my bicycle upright on the ridges separating the rice paddies was difficult, and walking alongside my bike on the narrow ridges was almost impossible. Sometimes I slipped, but since the paddies were dry during the hot season, it was not a big deal – it just made the trip longer. During the hour-and-a-half trek to the village, I thought of my good fortune at being a Peace Corps Volunteer in Thailand. The people of the Northeast were very friendly and gracious. They welcomed me into their homes and shared their food. I had been told during orientation in Bangkok that the Northeast was a hotbed of communist infiltration from Laos, but I never sensed any animosity during my two-year stay.

My trip to Vang Village was a direct result of moving from the Teacher Training College residence to my new home near the Trade School. It was Charoon and Luk who had earlier taken me to Vang Village to meet their friends. They went out of their way to teach me about Northeast Thailand village life, and to introduce me to people outside my immediate circle of colleagues and friends in Udorn. I was growing and learning in Thailand as I had envisioned when I volunteered for the Peace Corps in March 1961.

After bicycling and walking about an hour and a half, I arrived at the village. When the children saw me, they came running and waied deeply. ("Waied" means to bow and put the hands together as in prayer.) They remembered me from my earlier visit, but I was still an oddity – maybe the first white person (falang) to visit their village . . . and one who spoke some Lao dialect. I was something of a celebrity, as were other volunteers in the first Peace Corps groups, especially those who lived outside the larger cities.

I was pleased to be in the partial shade of the village, set among scattered coconut and fruit trees. The houses were on stilts to keep them dry during the rainy season. This had the salutary effect of providing ample air circulation throughout the house and creating something akin to, but not quite, a cool breeze. I found the traditional Thai home comfortable, even during the hot season.

Mr. Kasem, Vang's Headman, invited me and

the villagers who had gathered in his home to enjoy his gracious hospitality. The Mekong whiskey and sticky rice and spicy fish sauce were laid out on a woven grass mat, and we squatted on the floor in a circle around the food. I rolled the sticky rice into a ball between my thumb and fingers, dipped it in the "hot" sauce, and ate it with a sip of Mekong. I was tired after my long trek in the heat, and I was hungry for this treat. I enjoyed the sticky rice, the whiskey, the conversation about family and friends, and about my life in Thailand. They were curious about me and my reaction to them: "Do you like Thailand? Can you eat our spicy food? Is Thailand too hot for you? Are Thai women beautiful? Do you want a Thai woman?"

"I love Thailand. Your food is delicious. The weather is not too hot for me and yes, Thai women are very beautiful." But I declined their offer of a woman, "I have a girlfriend back home." They didn't always believe my answers, and thought I was just being polite when I said Thai women were very beautiful. They thought the lighter-skinned women (men too) of Northern Thailand, particularly those from Chiengmai, were much more beautiful than the darker-skinned women of Northeast or Southern Thailand. They thought any white-skinned person more beautiful than any dark-skinned person.

This thinking was new to me. The people of Lille, Maine, were the opposite of diverse: we were Catholic, French, and white. An African American or Asian American coming through Lille in the 1950s was a rare event which attracted much attention – an oddity, same as I was in Vang. Living in Thailand lifted the veil from my eyes and helped me see through the cracks of my culture.

The Thais love conversation, have great fun playing with words, changing their usual meanings to entertain each other. They sang and asked me to sing too – it didn't make any difference that I didn't have a good singing voice. As my language skills improved, I joined in the repartee, the jokes, and the play on words. I found this way of entertainment not very different from my growing-up-days in Lille when televisions were few, movie houses were distant, and entertainment was something we did for ourselves among family and friends.

Upon arriving in the village, I had noticed a few babies who looked ill and listless on their mothers' hips or lying in makeshift small hammocks. While eating and drinking, I saw more small babies who were sick. I asked one of the mothers, "What's wrong with your baby?"

"Our babies are sick. We don't know what to do. Can you help?"

"I don't know anything about medicine, and don't think I can do anything to help your babies. I'm not a doctor."

More out of curiosity than anything else, I asked if I could touch the babies on their foreheads to check their temperatures. (In Thailand people do not normally touch the upper part of a person's body because they believe that's their most divine part. This is less so for a baby or small child, but I didn't want to take a chance on offending by touching the forehead of a baby without permission.) I could tell that the babies had very high temperatures, but that's all I could tell. I had a few pamphlets on tropical disease at my home in Udorn, and without saying it, I resolved to try to do something for the babies upon my return.

After eating too much sticky rice and drinking too much Mekong, I left the village and reached home by early evening, to the relief of my host families.

During my return trek, I thought of asking for help from a U.S. Marine doctor I had met in Udorn's small Catholic Church. He was part of a contingent of about twelve hundred Marines ordered to Udorn by President John Kennedy to "send a message" to the Pathet Lao – communists in nearby Laos. The Marines were camped near the small Udorn airport, also used as a base for Air America – the CIA's air force – which flew regularly to the jungles of Laos, but that's another story.

I had stayed away from the Marine camp because I was afraid to be identified with the military and the CIA. However, the disturbing images of the sick babies made me break my rule. I went to the camp, told the Marine doctor about the babies, and asked if he could go to the village with me. He could not leave his post, nor could he diagnose the illness from what I had told him, but he gave me a large jar of aspirins saying, "It won't hurt the babies and might help them by lowering their body temperatures."

The next day, I returned to the village with my large jar of aspirins. I had tied the jar with elastic cords to the carrier over the rear wheel of my bike, but it kept slipping, and I had to stop often to tighten the cords. It took me a long time to reach Vang. Mr. Kasem, the village Headman, and the other villagers were surprised to see me again so soon.

I told them I had some medicine and that maybe, just maybe, it might lower the babies' temperatures and help heal them. We split the adult-size aspirin tablets in half, and I gave about ten days' worth of tablets to the mothers for each sick baby. I instructed them on the dosage, the number of times each day, and told them to give the medicine until it ran out.

While returning to Udorn, a new worry came to me: "What if one or more of the babies die? Will they blame me for the death or deaths?" Maybe what I had done was not such a good idea. I feared the unknown reaction of the villagers should a baby die, and I thought of the harm potential publicity about this might have on the young Peace Corps. My fears were unjustified, as most fears are. A few weeks later when I returned to the village, I found a bunch of healthy babies. Mr. Kasem and the other villagers greeted me very warmly, thanked me, and gave me too much credit for saving their babies. I emphasized that their babies had gotten better because of the great care they had lavished on them, but they insisted, "Your medicine saved our babies." This was an occasion for celebration, and they brought out the sticky rice, spicy fish sauce, and Mekong whiskey.

I felt Tom Dooleyish. Dr. Tom Dooley, who had attended the University of Notre Dame and the University of St. Louis Medical School, had become very famous for his work in North Vietnam and Laos in the 1950s. He had written a number of popular books about his work setting up hospitals, and ministering to the health needs of many people in remote Laotian villages. He was considered a forerunner of Peace Corps Volunteers by many people. I was inspired by his life and work. He died of cancer in his early thirties. Later, in a more cynical time, the sheen of his accomplishments and adventures was considerably dulled.

I climbed the stairs to Mr. Kasem's home, squatted with the other men around the rice, fish sauce, and Mekong whiskey while the women prepared more food for the feast. This celebration was going to last a while, so I paced myself with the Mekong. There was always a thing about trying to get the falang (foreigner) tipsy, if not drunk.

We talked and joked and laughed. They wondered how hard it must be for me to be away from my family. It was difficult for them to understand why I would leave my rich country. (Sometimes a mother would offer her baby to me to take to America for a better life. I had a hard time believing she was serious.) I told them I loved my country, that we had poor people in America too, and that I appreciated the benefits and beauty of the Thais and their way of life. I told them I missed my family and friends, but I had a new large family here. I said that learning their language and culture, their enjoyable conversations, their play on words, and their great sense of humor made my life with them very good. Still, it was difficult for them to understand me and the culture of volunteerism from which I came.

Meanwhile, the women had killed a duck or rooster, I forget which, for a special treat. While it was being cooked, the wife of the village Headman, Mrs. Kasem, brought the blood drawn from the duck or rooster to drink with our whiskey. The men took the glass of raw blood, spiked it with whiskey, and gave it to me for the first swig. Although, I ate and drank most everything in the villages and cities of Thailand, I declined this one special drink. I told them my stomach could not handle raw duck (or rooster) blood. They accepted my reason for they understood stomach aches very well – a too common malady in the village. That was the only time I refused a food or drink during my time in Thailand. I can still see that glass of raw blood. It looked like tomato juice.

WILD RIDE IN A HELICOPTER
WITH SARGENT SHRIVER

I was in a helicopter with Sargent Shriver to visit volunteers in Khorat, about a one-hour ride from Udorn. It was an American-made helicopter, maybe a precursor of the ubiquitous Hueys of the Vietnam War – I'm not sure of the make or model. I sat on a bench facing Sargent Shriver and a couple of his assistants, and next to me were Art and Jack, volunteers at the Udorn Teacher Training College, and Dave, another volunteer whom Shriver had invited for the ride. We strapped ourselves into our seats and, at Sargent Shriver's suggestion, the door was left wide-open to let cool air rush past our faces as we were lifted above Udorn. I hadn't felt air this cool since I had left Maine eight months earlier in October, 1961.

This was the rainy (monsoon) season – early June, I think – and it was hot and humid and wet and green. It was around noon on a sunny day with only a few clouds, but that could change suddenly, since it's in the nature of monsoons to arise that way. I wasn't thinking of possible storms as I watched the countryside passing by like a movie through the open door in front of me; I was in awe of the miracle wrought by the rains that had colored the dusty brown landscape in every shade of green, had filled rice paddies with water, had flooded homes and villages, and had turned dirt roads to mud. I could almost see the frustration on the face of the bus driver below trying to get his bus free, and I could almost see the satisfaction on the faces of a woman and her children tending rice plants in the rice paddy.

Earlier that day, Sargent Shriver had visited my home and school, and I had introduced him to my host families and colleagues. He had removed his shoes before entering my home, had worn the heavy blue cotton shirt (closed at the front with cotton ties) of the Thai farmer, given him by my students, and had tried to play the Khaen (Northeast bamboo flute). Shriver embodied the Peace Corps spirit in his respect for the people's culture and language and feelings. That's why he had asked for a Thai pilot and helicopter to visit volunteers – unlike the American Ambassador, who accompanied him in an American military helicopter.

Sargent Shriver's way of running the Peace Corps was hands on – he visited us, and talked with our colleagues and principals. In Washington, he got theory, made policy, and kept Congress happy. In Thailand and Nigeria and Chile – the early Peace Corps countries – he saw volunteers in action. In the helicopter he said, "Peace Corps is a work in progress, you volunteers are creating the Peace Corps, not me, not the staff."

Shriver peppered us with questions: "How's your health? Are you lonely? Do you think you're making a difference? Should we send more volunteers to Udorn? Do you feel needed here?"

"I feel we're making a real difference," Art said. "The students are very hungry to learn English and to find out about us and about America. Our students are going to be teachers in the elementary and high schools, so our impact will be substantial and long term."

I said, "I'm teaching English as a second language at two schools, and I'm organizing the library and helping the carpentry teacher, but my carpentry teaching job is not highly needed. I think other volunteers should be assigned to Udorn and the Northeast, but not as teachers of carpentry."

While we were talking, I noticed the sky clouding and the wind increasing; I thought we might be in for a storm. No sooner had that thought passed, than the rains came. We quickly closed the door, and our helicopter was almost immediately engulfed by a monsoon storm of torrential rains and bluish-black clouds which turned the bright midday sky into midnight darkness. Typhoon gusts threw us like a cork in rough seas, and when our helicopter wasn't being pulled up and let down like a yo-yo, it slid on air this way and that, like a sled on ice. Lightning pierced the stormy darkness, and thunder punctuated the noise of our groaning helicopter as it twisted in corkscrew winds and pelting rain.

I had seen military helicopters fly over Udorn, and had often thought it would be fun to ride one. Now I wasn't so sure. As long as Sargent Shriver sitting across from me remained calm and serene, I remained calm and serene. But when I saw our pilot struggling to keep the helicopter stable and upright, and the conversation ebbed, and Shriver's face showed concern, I was concerned, too. I didn't want to die in a helicopter – not even with the President's brother-in-law.

My concern grew and I became frightened when our helicopter dropped in what seemed a free fall. I couldn't see anything and I thought the pilot couldn't either. I resigned myself to a swift death in a Thai military helicopter in the middle of a rice paddy. Suddenly, maybe a hundred feet from the ground, the pilot yanked the helicopter to a hover, looked around, and quickly brought it down in a flooded field, not far from a water buffalo and an old shed whose faint outline he had seen.

The pilot opened the door. I rolled up the legs of my pants and jumped into knee-high water amidst rice shoots, in my Sunday shoes. I didn't know where we were, and neither did the others. We had been blown off-course, and even the pilot wasn't sure where we were. As we stood in the water with rain pelting us and lightning and thunder scaring us we noticed a farmer and his children, whom we had surprised by dropping from the sky, walking slowly toward us. They had been lured out of the old shed in the rain to take a closer look at this extraordinary scene unfolding in their rice paddy. We met them halfway to the shed and Art, who was the best speaker of the local Lao dialect (our pilot was from Bangkok and didn't know that dialect) asked the farmer, "Where are we? What's the name of the closest town?"

"The closest town is Konkhaen, about a day's walk from here."

Meanwhile, Shriver was having a great time kibitzing in everyman's language with the children, playing the role of a Peace Corps Volunteer as he imagined it. The farmer invited us out of the wind-whipped rain to the shed and I told the farmer that Sargent Shriver was Director of the Peace Corps and President Kennedy's brother-in-law – an important U. S. Government official.

He found that hard to believe, asking, "If he's such a high official, why is he wearing a Thai farmer's shirt?"

Almost as soon as we took cover in the shed, the storm left – almost as quickly as it had arrived – and the sun shone brightly. After some quick goodbyes and deep wais we boarded our helicopter. In about 20 minutes we were in Khorat, where Thai dignitaries and volunteers were anxiously waiting for us. The American Ambassador and his entourage were nowhere in sight; they had not yet arrived.

That evening, while having a meal of curries, steamed vegetables, rice spiked with fish sauce, Mekong whiskey and Singha beer, we learned that the Ambassador's helicopter had run out of fuel while being tossed about by the storm, and had been forced to land far from us. Our pilot had picked them up and flown them to Bangkok, leaving their helicopter and pilot in the rice fields where they had landed. Now that we knew they were safe, Shriver joked, "Our Thai pilot was more skilled than the Ambassador's." He kidded about the Ambassador's and his assistants' stuffiness, and bemoaned the tendency of American diplomats to live in "foreign enclaves" apart from the people.

Shriver discouraged the high-falutin receptions, consistent with his celebrity status as President Kennedy's brother-in-law that the host governments and embassies wanted for him. He was a good example for volunteers with his folksy approach, with the dignity and respect he treated ordinary citizens of Thailand, and with his trust in their intelligence and judgment. We were inspired by Shriver and I think he was inspired by us. President Kennedy had signed the legislation establishing the Peace Corps, but Sargent Shriver was its founder and inspiration.

WE CANNOT MAKE TRUCKS AND TRAINS, BUT WE CAN MAKE BABIES

It felt cold in tropical Udorn that morning. It was the cold season when temperatures can be as low as 50 degrees F at night warming to the upper 60s or lower 70s during the day. These temperatures, almost perfect in my Northern Maine home, felt cold when dressed in light clothes suitable for the 90- and 100-degree temperatures of the hot and wet Thailand seasons. I had awakened in the middle of the night shivering under my mosquito net, and had piled on all my clothes over the thin sheet to keep warm. I had gotten up earlier than usual because of the cold, had dressed quickly in layers, and had bicycled fast to school to keep warm.

The principal and teachers were gathered on the school's long veranda, sitting where the morning sun shone brightly – not in the shade where they sat during the very hot days. While they were sipping their hot coffee, spiked liberally with canned milk and sugar, they talked spiritedly about something I could not immediately grasp. I asked in Thai, "What are you talking about?"

"Oh, a train hit a big truck," answered my principal, Pricha.

"Was anyone hurt?" I asked. They all laughed.

"Why are you laughing?"

"We're not laughing at you, we're laughing because the first question Thai people ask about an accident is not whether anyone was hurt or killed, but how much damage was done."

While I was thinking, "They don't put too much value on human life here," one of the teachers said, "We cannot make trucks and trains in Thailand, but we can make babies." They laughed again, somewhat embarrassed, for they probably had a hint of what I was thinking.

I had received extensive training in Thai language and culture for three months at the University of Michigan Peace Corps Training Center. But as good as the training was, it couldn't have prepared me for what lay ahead. Seeing myself through the eyes of my Thai friends and colleagues taught me much about myself, my culture and my country, and about Thailand and her people – more than I had learned during training. I came to understand that in the United States we, too, measure the value of human lives with the cost of things: The cost of clean air compared to the cost of good health, the cost of safe cars and other products compared to the cost of injuries and loss of human lives.   My instant reaction to the comment, "We cannot make trucks and trains, but we can make babies," was negative, but I learned through the honesty and directness of my friends and colleagues that the difference in our valuation and appreciation of human life was one of degree, not one of kind.

My two years in Thailand taught me about the value a society puts on human life when human life is abundant and cheap, and trucks and trains are scarce and expensive. I learned how my values had been conditioned and determined to a large extent by my society and culture and education. I learned I was a prisoner of my culture, and that it was a challenge to escape that prison.

VANG VILLAGE II–
ILLEGAL GUN IN MY HANDS

I never cared to handle guns. I didn't even hunt and fish in Lille, Maine, where I was surrounded by hunters and fishermen. Once I went hunting for small game, and couldn't bring myself to shoot any. Another time I went fishing, and couldn't bring myself to impale the worm on the fishhook – and thinking of the hook in the fish bothers me still. I'm not a pacifist, and would kill to defend my family and myself, but the idea of killing anything is repugnant to me.

One day when the rainy season took a break, I took a break too, and bicycled to Vang. I enjoyed bicycling to see the people in Vang, and from time to time, I returned to the village. My visits there were always an occasion for a party: Mr. Kasem, the Village Headman, would invite friends and neighbors for sticky rice, spicy fish sauce, Mekong whiskey, and good conversation.

It was difficult getting to Vang during the rainy season because the rice paddies were full of water, and the ridges on which I rode my bike were wet and slippery. I didn't fall, but the path leading to and from the rice paddies had been overrun by water in many places, and when

I arrived at the village, my shoes, socks, and pants were wet.

The villagers laughed at me for wearing those clothes: shoes and socks and long pants were a luxury in the village. Their regular clothes were pawkamas for men and sarong-type dresses for women. (A pawkama is a cloth about three by five feet which is wrapped around the waist and worn loosely; it can serve as a bathing suit and as a modesty shield while bathing.)

I kicked off my shoes, peeled off my wet socks, rolled up my wet pant legs, and squatted down in a circle with the men. (As usual, the women hung out together, apart from the men.) We ate sticky rice soaked in fish sauce and drank Mekong whiskey. I asked about the children's health, and we discussed the weather and the crops.

The talk turned to guns. One of the men who made handguns had brought one with him, and passed it around for us to admire. Showing me this illegal gun meant I had gained their trust because in those days – I don't know about today – ownership of guns in Thailand was tightly controlled.

In the 1960s, there was communist influence in Northeast Thailand from the Pathet Lao of Laos (and also from the People's Republic of China) which bordered Thailand for hundreds of miles. The Thai and United States governments were very concerned about this influence, and had undertaken major initiatives to counteract this perceived communist threat in the Northeast.

As the "illegal" gun was moving around, I tried to avoid handling it, but the owner was proud of this hand-made gun, and I had to take it in my hands. As I was admiring the well-crafted gun and complimenting the maker, I heard a slight commotion outside, and saw someone's head bobbing up the stairs. Suddenly, the room was full of nervousness. Sensing trouble, I tried to pass the gun to someone else, but no one wanted it. I was left holding the gun and did the only thing possible: I wedged it into the back of my pants.

Mr. Yom, District Officer, (Title: Nai Ampur) had decided to pay a visit to Vang. Maybe he had heard of an American visiting the village, and he wanted to join the party or, more likely, it was just an unplanned drop-in visit. As the situation unfolded, I too became full of nervousness; not only were Peace Corps Volunteers not allowed to have guns, but Thais in the Northeast caught with guns would have been suspected of being involved with communists.

Mr. Yom stayed for the party, sitting close to me since I was the "guest of honor." I didn't feel very honorable eating and drinking and talking with an illegal gun tucked in the back of my pants. I was eager for the District Officer to leave so I could get rid of this illegal gun. Meanwhile, I was thinking of the possible negative repercussions on Peace Corps of being found with a gun. Any incident, even a small one, could be magnified greatly and could hurt the Peace Corps. Earlier, there had been what became known as the postcard incident in Nigeria: a Peace Corps Volunteer had written a postcard home which contained less than complimentary remarks about the people of Nigeria. The incident had rocked the Peace Corps for a few weeks.

I needed to urinate, but didn't want to get up because the District Officer could have seen the gun tucked in my pants. The more I ate and drank, the more I needed to go to the bathroom; I was in pain when Mr. Yom finally left for the next village.

After Mr. Yom's departure, the nervousness left the room and left me too. We were all relieved. I was relieved of the gun, relieved in the bathroom, and relieved of my fears. Mr. Kasem and the gun owner were very thankful for my discretion, and I was very thankful I was not caught with the gun. It would have likely brought my Peace Corps Volunteer career to a premature end.

RAINMAKING IN UDORN

The rains were late and spare and water was scarce. Paddies of rice and patches of corn were suffocating. Mango trees were half-full and fish were dying in parched puddles; children grabbed fish and took them home for dinner. The chickens were scrawnier than chicken wire. Rice had to be imported from other parts of Thailand, using up precious cash. Unless ample rains came soon, the poorest would not have enough to eat, and the weakest in remote villages would suffer from malnutrition, maybe worse.

Some years ago in the United States, attempts were made to cause rain by flying planes above the clouds and sprinkling them with crystals of iodide. In Udorn, talk of making rain focused on using techniques and materials at hand – probably no more and no less arcane than sowing clouds with crystals of iodide. My colleagues at the Trade School decided to do something about the lack of rain by talking with the monks at the nearby wat (Buddhist Temple) about invoking the phi (spirit) of rain.

The rain ritual had not been done for a few years; maybe there had been sufficient rains or maybe these superstitions were losing favor with better educated persons.

My colleagues were not yet disentangled from these superstitions – and I suspected many other educated Thais still
believed in the phi of rain beneath their patina of sophisti-
cation.

The monks agreed to invoke the phi of rain.
They blessed the rice plants and chanted in the rice fields
morning and afternoon for three days. During these three
days, they were given only dry foods to eat and nothing
to drink – this was to make the monks suffer so the phi
of rain would have compassion for them and cause rain
to fall. On the fourth day, the monks were served a lav-
ish breakfast and lunch. Late that afternoon after school,
teachers, students, and many other persons formed a long
procession led by one member dressed as a large female
cat, and for good measure, a real live female cat followed
right behind the made-up cat. The procession went from
house to house to collect funds for the monks who had
fasted and chanted for three days.

As the searing sun slipped below the horizon, the
monks left for their wat, and we continued on our serpen-
tine way, drinking, swaying, singing, and dancing to the
rhythm of drums. Later, the ritual ended and the festivities
over, I returned home hoping for rain, but not expecting
any. There had been no clouds in the sky for days and the
stars shone bright that night as I crawled in bed under my
mosquito net.

What time it was I'm not sure; it must have been
the dead of night, for no one in the house was stirring, but
through the grogginess of half-awakeness and the after-
effects of rice whiskey, I heard our tin roof responding to
tiny, tentative drops of rain. I thought I was dreaming, but
those tiny and tentative drops soon morphed into dollops
of rain drumming with increasing frequency here and
there on the roof. Then it came, the deafening noise of
a monsoon rain, whipped by winds, turning our tin roof

into a giant megaphone. We're all up and wide awake – kids, cats, dog, and all.

This has to be a coincidence: I can't believe that chanting and fasting, a made-up female cat and a real female cat, and a parade had caused this torrential rain. I'm a skeptic, a "modern man." I believe in science and cause and effect and seeing to believe. When my colleagues had talked about spirits invading the bodies of sick people or about the power of the small spirit house near each home to ward off evil spirits, or when they had warned me about passing close by wats late at night, I had listened politely, but I had not taken them seriously. When they had talked about invoking the phi to make rain, I had been interested and had wanted to participate, but I didn't believe.

I thought I was above those simple beliefs and practices. Today, I regret my naïveté and my barely disguised feelings of cultural superiority. I'm humbled to think I could not see the connection and the parallel between the Thais' beliefs in spirits and my beliefs in spirits and rituals. My Catholic religion, which I practiced fervently then, is permeated with the language of spirits, souls, saints, and guardian angels; it's full of rituals.

I prayed to God and saints for many things: healing, a job, and good health for my family. I participated in blessings of potato crops and attended a Mass in my brother-in-law's potato storage so his crop wouldn't spoil and would sell for a good price. I used many rituals and amulets. I invoked St. Anthony to find something lost; I had my throat blessed with a St. Blaise candle to keep my throat healthy; I had St. Christopher medals in my cars to ward off accidents; I prayed with my father to St. Jude, the patron saint of carpenters; and I invoked my guardian angel to guide and protect me.

I don't believe in spirits and saints and angels and rituals as I did when I was younger, nor do I believe in spirits as my Udorn colleagues did decades ago. But I believe in forces I can't see or measure, forces that can't be quantified by science; I believe in the existence of unknown forces which operate in the world we see and in the world we don't see. I didn't know then that I knew very little.

Maybe it was a coincidence that it rained in Udorn after the phi of rain was invoked. Maybe not.

THE RACE TO SAKOLNAKORN

The big bus converted from a truck did not leave on time. Buses rarely left on the posted hour and drivers always tried to make up lost time by driving too fast. We were squeezed so tightly in the bus I didn't think we could jam in one more chicken or one more pig or one more bunch of bananas or one more person, but when a woman showed up with a small child and a big bag, a young man gave up his seat inside, sat outside on the roof with the baggage and sundry goods, and we sucked in our stomachs to help her fit in. Filling buses beyond capacity was an economic necessity like overfilling airplanes today.

I was on my way to Sakolnakorn to visit two newly-arrived volunteers at the request of the Peace Corps staff in Bangkok, and the bus was the only way to get there. I enjoyed the bus for the cheek-by jowl humanity of it, but riding the bus was dusty, tiring, and risky. Dirt roads were narrow and rutty; buses were not well-maintained, and bus drivers were not well trained. They drove too fast and took too many risks. Bus drivers seemed to enjoy the thrills of tailgating, passing blind on hills, and racing other buses. Riding a bus was like being in a race on the Indianapolis 500 Speedway with no cautionary yellow lights.

Finally, our driver was satisfied he could not pile in another passenger or bundle and we were set to go a full hour after our scheduled departure. The engine sputtered, cleared its throat, and powered its ungainly load down the road, spewing black diesel smoke and raising a cloud of dust behind us. We rolled slowly in the city, but when we reached the edge of Udorn, the driver gunned the engine. Never mind the ruts in the road or the water buffalo pulling a cart or the kids playing nearby, we were going to make it to Sakolnakorn on time.

I was sitting in the back of the bus – I always sat in the back of the bus because I thought that was the safest place to be. Not that I dwelled on the dangers, but getting on the bus meant I had decided to put my life in the hands of the driver, and there was no use fretting about it.

There was more than one bus leaving for Sakolnakorn and beyond that busy morning. Soon after we left, I noticed one slowly gaining on us. At first our driver didn't seem to be paying attention to the other bus, but when it got closer, I could tell he was trying to keep a calculated distance ahead of it.

Ours was a burly bus, lumbering but strong, slow to pick up speed, but good at hurling itself down the road with a heavy load. Its sides were painted with red and yellow flames seemingly streaming from the engine, undulating to the rear, creating an illusion of speed and daredevilism. Softening this fiery image was a peaceful-looking Buddha-like ornament on the hood to fend off evil spirits.

We were on a long stretch of level road and our bus was able to stay ahead of its come-from-behind competition, but when we started to climb a long hill, the other bus gained on us and slowly nosed alongside. I could see that this bus was slightly shorter than ours, had a smaller load, and seemed more sprightly – an advantage over our larger heavily loaded bus.

When a water buffalo appeared on our side of the road with its boy handler, we had to slow down, and the competition pulled ahead. Chicken feathers flew, the pigs squealed, the passengers yelled, and those on top of the bus held on for dear life. Young men shouted to our driver the Thai equivalent of "slam the pedal to the metal," but the other bus had gotten the better of us going up the hill and we were eating its dust as it lurched precariously, barely avoiding the ditch, and landing in the middle of the road. The driver and passengers in the other bus were laughing and waving at us. We were losing face.

The race had been firmly engaged, and we were in for an exciting ride. Our driver knew the roads and his bus intimately. After we topped the hill, he gunned his engine to the fullest, achieving maximum speed downhill to take advantage of the flywheel effect our greater weight and speed would give for the next hill to climb. We caught up with our competition at the base of the hill, and when our momentum kicked in and the road widened, we passed the other bus, steered in front, and greedily straddled the middle of the narrow road to prevent it from passing us again, moving aside only to let oncoming vehicles go by.

Nervousness and fear appeared in the faces of some older passengers, but the younger passengers egged the driver on; loss of face had to be put off at all costs. There was no way our driver, who had started first in this "race," was going to arrive to Sakolnakorn last. He was not going to lose the lead again.

Now we were only about five or six miles from our first scheduled stop on the outskirts of Sakolnakorn, and our driver was still going at a suicidal speed and still straddling the middle of the road. The driver behind was moving to the right and to the left trying to pass, driving at a crazy speed, and doing so in blinding dust.

As we approached our first stop, our driver took

his foot off the accelerator, slammed the brakes, bringing our bus to an abrupt stop next to a small market full of people selling fried chicken parts, sticky rice, bananas, and assorted trinkets. Our dust caught up with us, engulfed us, and filtered into the crowd. Then I heard the loud roar of the other bus charging full speed through the market, its passengers and driver laughing and shouting and challenging us to race to the next town. People in the street scattered quickly out of the way.

A short distance ahead, through the veil of dust, I noticed an old man, head down, pedaling his bike directly toward the bus, and I saw the driver of the speeding bus looking behind at us, oblivious of the man on the bike. We yelled loudly, more out of horror than anything else, because nothing could have prevented this accident. The man on the bike and the bus met head on. Instantaneously, it seemed, man and bike were fused into one mass that was lifted off the ground by the bus, pulled back to the ground by gravity, then dragged under the bus for hundreds of feet until the bus was able to stop.

Men, women, and children stumbled over each other to the scene of the accident. Commotion reigned until the police arrived, arrested the driver, and dragged him to jail – a good thing, because he might have been killed by the people in the street. No one did anything about the crumpled mass of man and bike under the bus.

While this grisly scene was unfolding, I was having an interior debate about my religious obligation in this situation: My Catholic Church had drilled into me that a person could not pass through the gates of heaven without being baptized in the Catholic faith. The man under the bus was no doubt a Buddhist – most Thais were. If I baptized him I would be sending him directly to heaven. If I didn't he would go to hell or to purgatory or to some other nebulous place; he would never be with God.

My religion told me to baptize the man, but my guts told me not to do so. I listened to my guts. I think it was my respect for Thais, their culture, and their religion which helped me prevail over the Catholic dogma taught me as a boy. I had witnessed the kindness, gentleness, and generosity of my Buddhist colleagues and friends, and I had been impressed. Their Buddhist beliefs seemed to influence their day-to-day behavior more than my Catholic beliefs did mine. They said, "Buddhism is more a way of life than an organized religion," and I believed it.

Sakolnakorn was my stop. I hired a samlow, and was pedaled by a young man to the home of the two volunteers I had taken the bus to visit.

UDORN TO HAWAII:
TRAINING VOLUNTEERS

It's September, 1963, and I'm thinking about what to do after my two years of service in Udorn. I considered seeking a one year extension of my service, which would have likely been approved, but I also wanted to go home to marry my girlfriend Rolande around the Christmas holidays, or not much later, so I ruled that out. Graduate studies or law school were options, but most intriguing was a motorcycle trip that my colleague, Art, (volunteer at the Teacher Training College in Udorn) and I had discussed. We had dreamed about a trip across Asia to the Middle East, down the East African coast to Madagascar to visit my mother's missionary cousin, Sister Abela, then up to England for a ship to New York.

While pondering my future, Peace Corps Thailand Director, Glenn Ferguson, told me that the University of Hawaii Hilo Peace Corps Volunteer Training Center wanted to hire a volunteer who had completed his service and who had served successfully. They were seeking former volunteers to help train volunteers for Thailand and other Southeast Asian countries. They wanted to make training more realistic, and to provide trainees with a real "live" model of a successful volunteer – something not available to the very first Peace Corps volunteers.

Ferguson suggested I contact the Training Center and that he would recommend me for the position. He had gotten to know me well, not only because of my two years of successful volunteer experience, but also because of my experience as a Volunteer Staff Assistant. A Volunteer Staff Assistant was something like a volunteer leader, but Ferguson had not wanted to use this title due to its implication of being "over other volunteers". Volunteers were seriously egalitarian, subject only to supervision by the host country institution, not by the Peace Corps country director or any other volunteer. I too did not want that title which I thought would get in the way of my duties to assist newer volunteers in their work.

Almost, immediately upon learning of my interest, and Ferguson's recommendation, the director of the Hilo Training Center offered me a training coordinator position, which I eagerly accepted. Not only would this position allow me to use my volunteer experience to make training more realistic, but as I realized later, it was a great transition from being a Peace Corps Volunteer to a "regular job." As the Peace Corps found out later, the transition to life back home for many volunteers who had been totally immersed in another culture for a few years, was not always easy.

Truth is I had very little money to buy a motorcycle and to finance months of travel, even on the cheap. All I had was the money set aside by Peace Corps – about $60 for each month of service – so volunteers wouldn't fall on welfare after their return to the United States, or as Peace Corps put it, "to help the volunteer transition to a job or studies." I had spent most of my monthly stipend. (I believed that my role was to leave as much money in the local economy as I could...not that the stipend provided much extra to save.)

I set out for Hawaii by way of Manila, Hong Kong, and Tokyo. Art extended his volunteer tour in Udorn and years later, married a Laotian woman in Vientiane. Months later, I married a French Acadian woman in Van Buren, Maine.

SMUGGLING THE RINGS

The lines were long and the customs officers in their uniforms were taking their good old time, rummaging in suitcases, digging in carry-ons, and looking in handbags at the Honolulu airport. Maybe it was the slow tropical rhythm of the islands in 1963 – a rhythm I had grown to enjoy in Thailand – or maybe the officers were serious about nabbing people who were trying to avoid the tariff on jewelry bought cheap in Asia.

I had waited in many lines in Udorn: I had waited in a line to purchase rice, I had waited in another line to pay for the rice, and I had waited in still another line for the rice to be bagged. I had waited for friends late for coffee and for students late for appointments. In America, time is not to be wasted. In Thailand, time is to be lived. I had learned to live time. I had learned to think about nothing. I had learned to be more intimate with my surroundings. I had learned to be patient; and when my patience had been overcome by my American desire to not waste time, I had given in and I had read many interesting books while waiting.

Still, I was antsy and fidgety. I was thinking about the diamond ring and wedding band I had in the watch pocket of those days' pants for which I didn't have the tariff money. I had bought the rings in Hong Kong for Rolande, an intelligent, warm, and sensual woman, for whom I had reconsidered more than once during the summer of 1961, my decision to join the Peace Corps. We had met in a bar in Van Buren, Maine, between college graduation and my departure for the Peace Corps, and we had fallen for each other immediately. By summer's end, we were in love and didn't want to part, but the adventure of Peace Corps had pulled me to Thailand, and she had understood. Our love for each other, nurtured through a two-year flurry of letters between Van Buren and Udorn, had deepened and I was ready to ask her to marry me.

The line slowed down, and when it came to the tall, blonde, early-30s lady in front of me, the officer seemed to get more meticulous about his work. He scrutinized everything inside her three suitcases and the bag she'd carried on the plane, then he said, "Please empty your handbag on the table and remove your jacket."

"Why?" she said. "You didn't ask the man in front of me to take off his jacket."

"It's my job lady. I have to check everything." He looked into the depths of her large handbag, then felt the lining of her jacket. A hint of a grin lit his face. His work had paid off. He discovered a cache of fine jewelry in the lining of her jacket, and turned her over to his supervisor. He signaled me to move up. By then, I was barely maintaining my composure. Not only was I nervous about the rings, I was nervous about my nervousness, thinking he might see through the nonchalance I was faking.

Not declaring the rings at customs was just a small jump from smuggling cigarettes across the border into New Brunswick, Canada, which I did as a teenager. I would buy cigarettes at Lawrence's General Store in Lille where I worked (without Lawrence's knowledge), put the cartons in boxes, tie the boxes to a sled, pull it across the St. John River on two-foot-thick ice, and sell them for a profit at a small store in Thibodeau. I would have a snack, drink a coke, and return home a little richer. When my parents got suspicious about my spending, and I wouldn't tell them about my smuggling, my brother Richard told them. They must have speculated I was stealing money, because when they learned the source of my extra cash, they were relieved.

I handed the officer my passport, which had been stamped by authorities in Thailand, Hong Kong, the Philippines, and Japan. "What were you doing in Southeast Asia?"

"I was a Peace Corps Volunteer teacher in Thailand."

He looked me over carefully and smiled. "Good work." He waved me on. No rummaging in my suitcases, no checking the lining of my jacket, no emptying of my watch pocket. The magic aura of the Peace Corps had protected me from my small smuggling crime.

DRAFT BOARD CLERK VS. ME, REVISITED

I arrived in the small city of Hilo on the Big Island in September 1963, and straightaway wrote a long letter to Rolande asking her to marry me. I wrapped the letter around the small box of the diamond ring I'd smuggled in and mailed it to Van Buren, Maine. The diamond was pure and clear like North Pole ice. It was not large; I had specified to the jeweler in Hong Kong that the whiteness and clearness of the diamond were more important than its size. I was not buying it for show, I was buying it for its beauty – a beauty I'd hoped would match Rolande's.

Next, I notified the clerk to Local Draft Board #2 in Caribou, Maine, of my new address in Hilo. That was the rule then: When a man of military draft age moved from one place to another, he had to notify his draft board. The clerk had much power over me; she had stood in the way of my teaching job in Nigeria and had only allowed me to be a volunteer teacher in Thailand at the Peace Corps' insistence. Still, I wasn't too concerned about being drafted: I was almost 25 years old; the War in Vietnam was small in 1963; and the Department of Defense was not drafting many men my age.

My letter and the diamond ring had flown to Van

Buren, Maine extra fast and so did the return mail which brought me Rolande's answer: "Yes," she said, "I will marry you."

I was ecstatic. A few colleagues had planted small doubts in me when they had emphasized I was nuts to think this beautiful woman (I had shown them a picture of Rolande) was still waiting for me after two years – they were joking, but only half.

In letters, we decided on a wedding date during the Christmas-New Year holidays when I would be home for the first time in two years. Rolande had her picture taken for the newspaper to announce our engagement, and she planned for the banns to be announced in St. Bruno's Catholic Church in Van Buren. We were on track to be married on her birthday, December 28. It would be cold in Northern Maine, but no worry, we would find a way to keep warm.

Rolande's yes wasn't the only mail. A few weeks later, I was ordered by the clerk to the draft board to be in Caribou, Maine for induction in the Armed Services just a few short weeks hence. The clerk had not forgotten me, and when she received my new address, she quickly prepared my orders and mailed them to me in Hilo, Hawaii.

I wasn't sure what to do. I felt it was my duty to serve my country in the military, yet I wanted to marry Rolande, and I didn't feel I could ask her to wait another two years while in the Army, likely in Thailand or Vietnam. I didn't want to be 12,000 miles away from Rolande for another two years. We loved each other, and after two years of being apart, we wanted to be together.

In Hilo, I shared an office with my supervisor, Dr. Collier, a University of Hawaii professor, who had served in the Army in the Philippines during World War II, had married a Filipina, and was now teaching the cultures of Southeast Asia to Peace Corps Volunteers (trainees). Dr.

Collier had become my mentor and friend, so I shared my dilemma with him. I told him I felt an obligation to fulfill my military obligation, but much more, I wanted to marry Rolande and to be with her.

"Roger," he said, "We need you here to help train volunteers more than the military needs you. Furthermore, there's an easy way out of your quandary; you've been out of the country too long. Don't you know that if you're married, you won't get called? They don't draft married men these days. Go home and get married."

I got on the phone immediately. It was a big deal and expensive to use the phone for long-distance calls from Hawaii in those days, but time was short – I had only two weeks left before my induction date. This was late Friday afternoon and I couldn't reach Rolande because she was in Connecticut for the weekend, so I called my mother and Rolande's mother to tell them of the change in plans. Then I made reservations to fly to New York City the next day. With $50 of borrowed cash (today's credit cards and ATMs were in the future) I got on an Aloha plane for Honolulu, spent too much money on a good meal in the airport, and waited for the Pan Am night flight to take off.

When I arrived at LaGuardia Airport in New York City, I wrote a check for a ticket to Hartford, Connecticut, and called my sister Priscille, who lived there, to meet me at Bradley Airport. She fed me, gave me a bed, and loaned me money for a bus ticket to Bangor, Maine, where Rolande was now working. I arrived at her friends' place, where she rented a room, before she returned from her weekend jaunt in Hartford. She had been told I was coming, but didn't expect to see me in her room when she arrived – she was most surprised.

Wedding banns were announced one Sunday instead of the usual three, and we were married on Saturday, November 30. We had a festive dinner and dance at the

Hammond Hotel, where we had met the summer of 1961. On Monday morning, December 2, I reported to the clerk in Caribou marriage license in hand. The clerk looked at me and said I was free to go. That was all.

We had a long honeymoon drive from Lille, Maine to Los Angeles, California, put our four-door-hardtop black Corvair with fancy wheels on a ship for Hawaii, and flew to Hilo for another adventure.

AUTHOR BIOGRAPHY

ROGER PARENT is a Trustee of the South Bend, Indiana School Board. He is a founder and President of World Dignity, Inc., a nonprofit organization with programs and activities in Thailand, India, and South Bend, Indiana.

Roger was one of the first Peace Corps Volunteers. He served in Thailand Group 1 for two years ending in August, 1963. He was also Director of Peace Corps in Haiti and Grenada in the late 1980's. He served South Bend, Indiana, as Councilman 8 years and as Mayor 8 year.

Roger was born in Lille, Maine. He attended elementary school in Lille, and was salutatorian of his class at Van Buren Boys High School (Maine). He earned a Bachelor degree, Magna Cum Laude, in Economics, from St. Francis Xavier University, Nova Scotia, (1961) and a Master's degree in Education from the University of Notre Dame (1966)

Roger Parent and his spouse Rolande (Ouellette) Parent, (born in Van Buren, Maine) have four children and six grandchildren. They live in South Bend, Indiana.

Musée culturel du Mont-Carmel
Post Office Box 150
Lille, Maine 04746
November 21, 2012

Dear Roger,
I have had the pleasure of reading your Manuscript, "The Making
of a Peace Corps Volunteer: From Maine to
Thailand", and I have enjoyed it very much. The first part of the
manuscript, your formation in the Saint John Valley in Northern
Maine is the part that I am most able to relate to, as it is my home
also.   I found it to be very engaging and enlightening. You grew up
in the time when the Valley was in transition, after World War II.
The old folk culture was beginning to give in to modern pressures
and you were in the midst of it, trying to resolve being of a minority
culture, speaking a different language, and forging a life in a new
age. You took advantage of a new program (Peace Corps) based on
service to a people half way around the world from where you were
raised and had to resolve problems that arose from past experiences
radically different from those you grew up with.

I recommend this well thought out oeuvre to anyone who feels
tied into a situation they believe to be out of their control. Your
example acts as a way of coping with change and making it work
positively while giving service to others.

Thank you for honoring me with the chance to read this manuscript
before publication.

Sincerely,
Don Cyr, Founder & Director
Musee Culturel du Mont-Carmel
Lille. Maine

HAPPENINGS

1939, Born in Lille, Maine, of Noel Parent and Blanche
      Corbin Parent.

1945, First Year of School, Notre Dame du Mont Carmel,
      Lille, Maine.

1953, Lincoln High School, Grand-Isle. One – room / one –
      teacher high school.

1955, Matriculated to Van Buren Boys High School for
      Junior and Senior Years.

1957, Graduated from St. Francis Xavier University, Antigon
      ish, Nova Scotia, B.A., Economics, 1961.

1961, Peace Corps Volunteer, Thailand.

1963, Married Rolande Ouellette. We have four children, six
      grandchildren.

1964, University of Notre Dame Graduate School, Masters in
      education, 1966.

1967, Directed Volunteer Tutoring Program and Neighbor
      hood Centers.

1971, Elected South Bend City Councilman; served 8 years.

1979, Elected Mayor of South Bend; served 8 years.

1988, Director, Peace Corps Programs in Haiti and Eastern
      Caribbean.

1994, Director of Development, Priests of Holy Cross,
      Indiana Province.

2005, Crisis Corps Volunteer (Special Peace Corps Program),
      Deputy Director of the Tsunami Volunteer Center
      in Khao Lak, Thailand. Assisted victims of the
      December 26, 2004 Tsunami.

2006, Founded World Dignity, Inc., a nonprofit organization
      focused on educational programs.

2008, Elected Trustee of the South Bend Community School
      Corporation.